MAP SKILL
Work Book

Social Science

Covering all the Maps of NCERT History & Geography along with Coverage of CBSE Examinations' Questions

CBSE

ARIHANT PRAKASHAN (School Division Series)

ARIHANT PRAKASHAN (School Division Series)
All Rights Reserved

卐 **Administrative & Production Offices**

Regd. Office
'Ramchhaya' 4577/15, Agarwal Road, Darya Ganj, New Delhi -110002
Tele: 011- 47630600, 43518550; Fax: 011- 23280316

Head Office
Kalindi, TP Nagar, Meerut (UP) - 250002, Tel: 0121-7156203, 7156204

卐 Sales & Support Offices
Agra, Ahmedabad, Bengaluru, Bareilly, Chennai, Delhi, Guwahati, Hyderabad, Jaipur, Jhansi, Kolkata, Lucknow, Nagpur & Pune

卐 ISBN : 978-93-25790-42-1

PO No : TXT-XX-XXXXXXX-X-XX

Published by Arihant Publications (India) Ltd.

For further information about the books from Arihant,
log on to www.arihantbooks.com or email to info@arihantbooks.com

Follow us on    

Contents

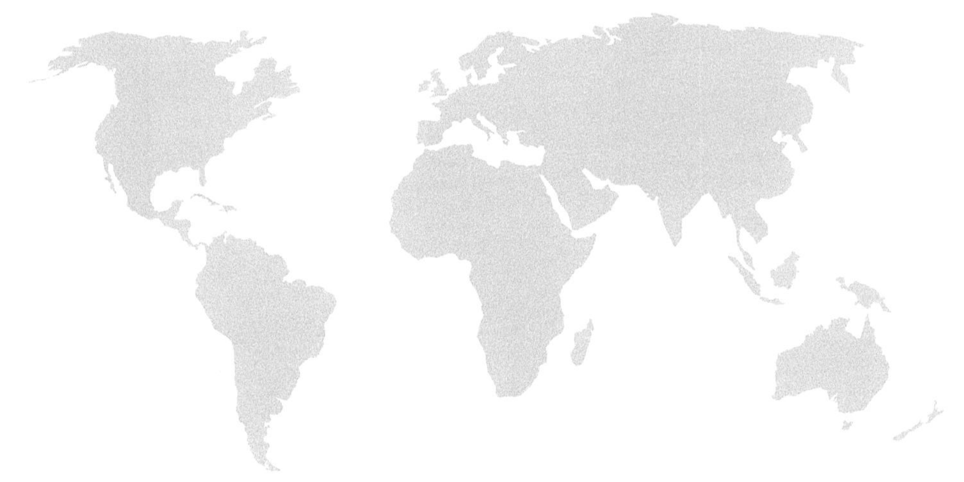

HISTORY

Important Sessions of Indian National Congress
(Chapter-2 Nationalism in India)

This map shows the Important Sessions of Indian National Congress from 1885 to 1947.

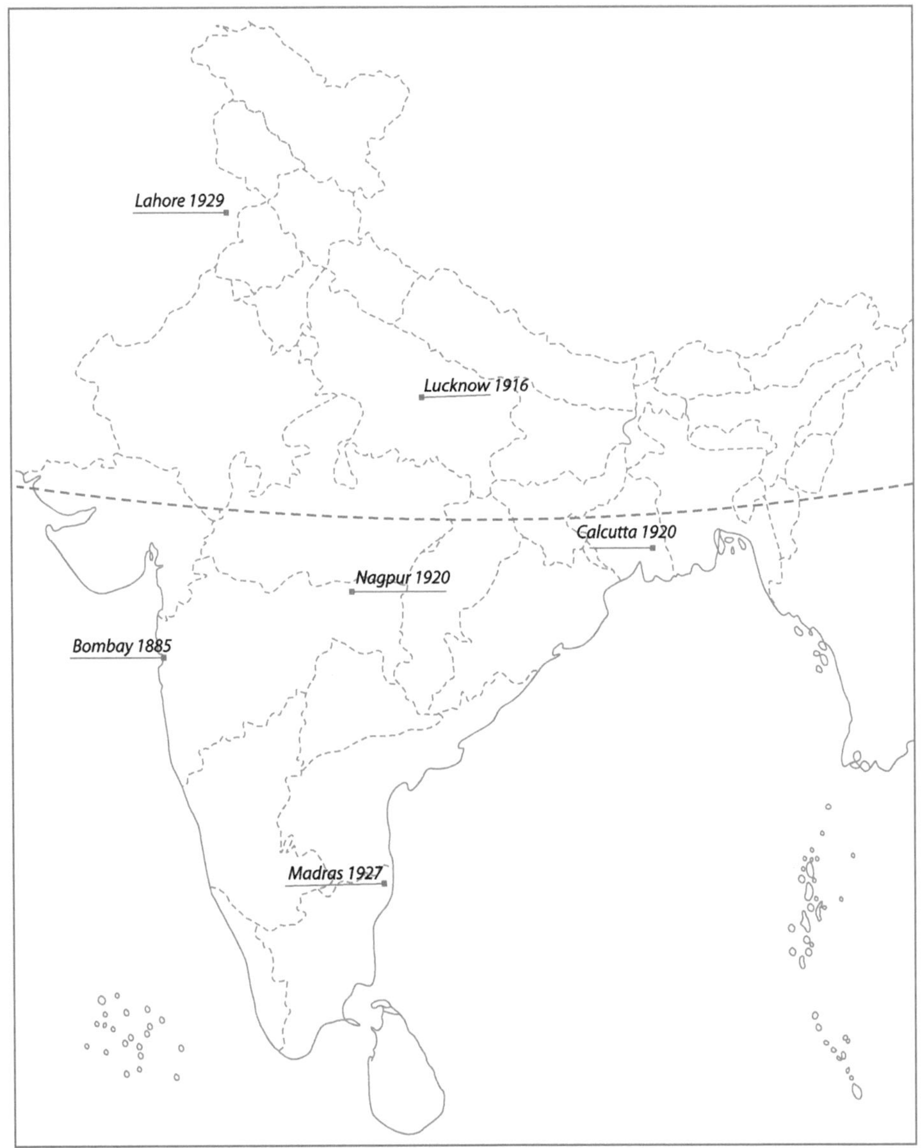

Practice Map 1

 Locate and label the following items on the given map

  1 Madras 1927   2 Nagpur 1920   [CBSE 2020]   3 Calcutta 1920

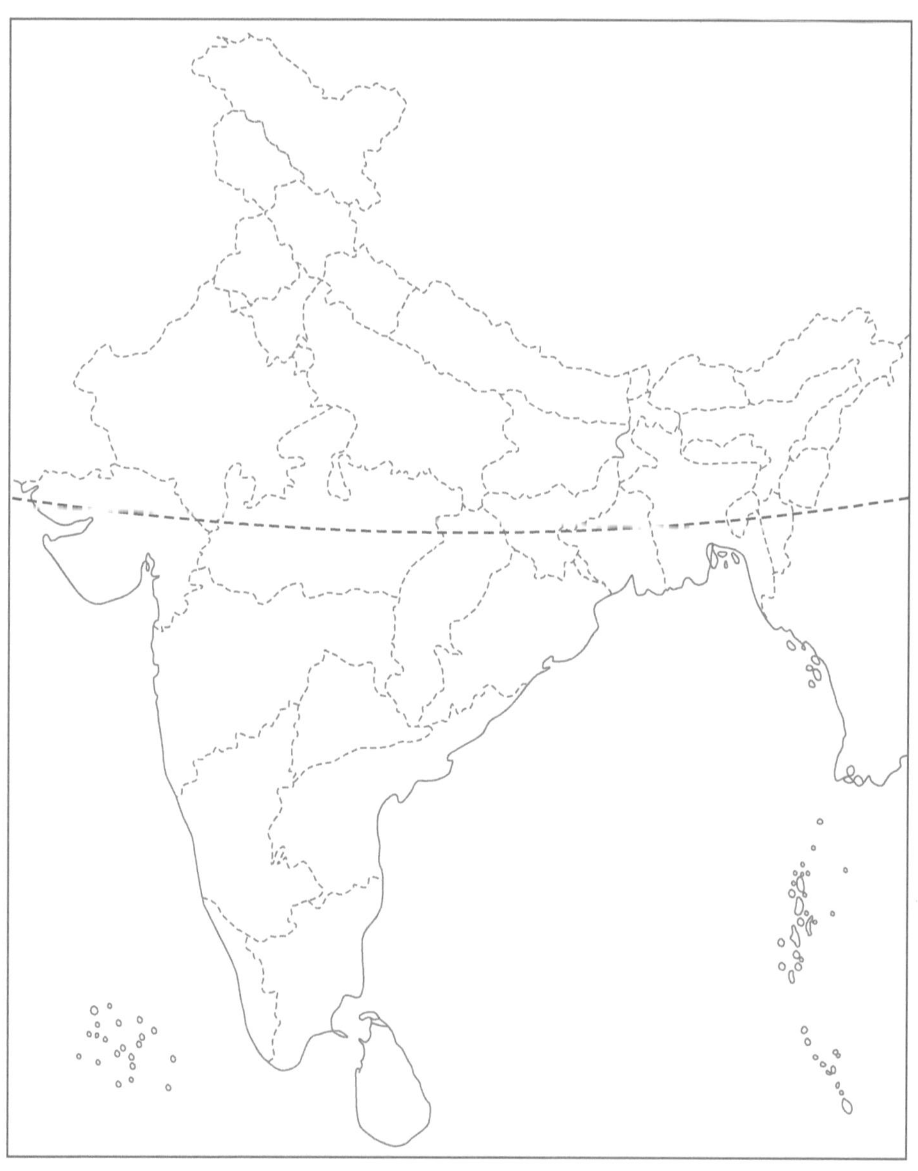

Important Centres of Freedom Movement in India
(Chapter-2 Nationalism in India)

This map shows the important centres of freedom movement in India from 1857 to 1947.

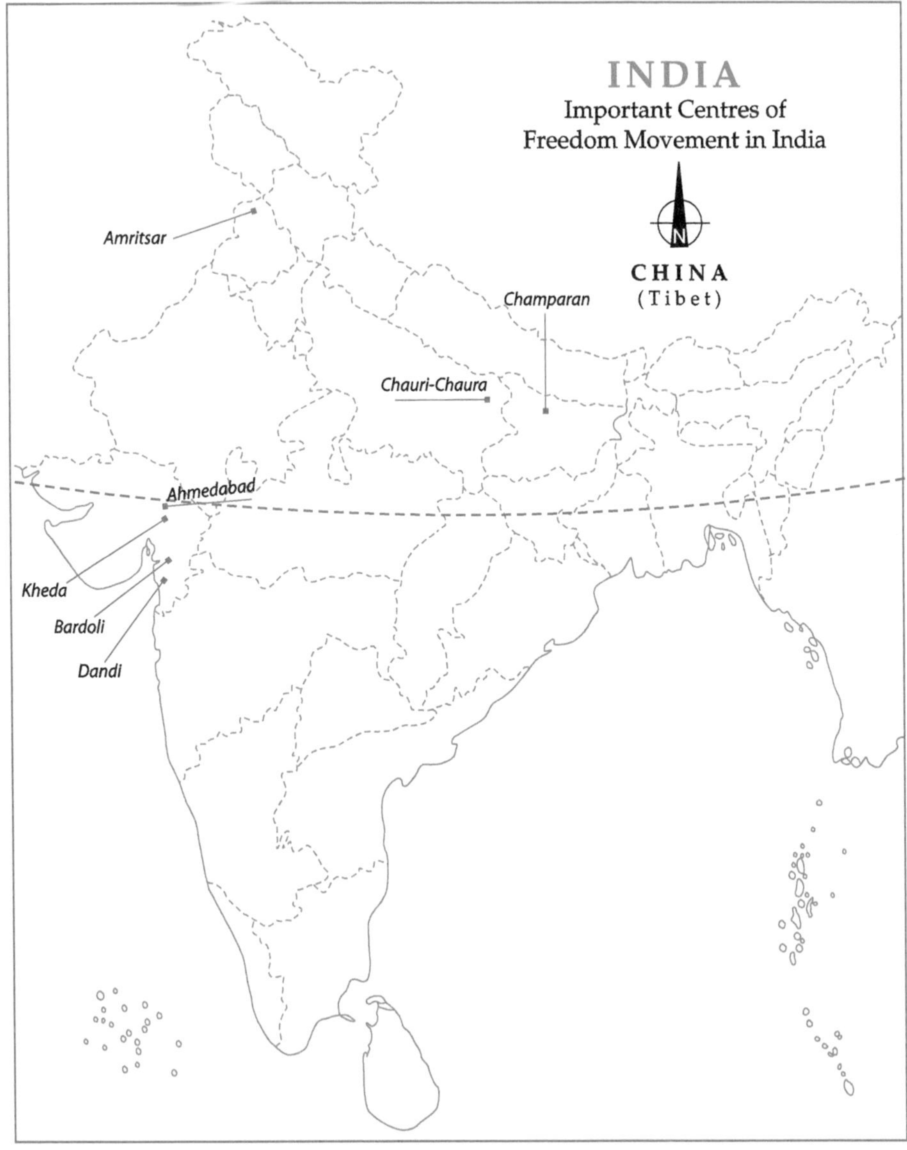

Practice Map 2

Q 2 Features are marked by numbers in the given political map of India. Identify these features with the help of the following information and write their correct names on the lines marked in the map.

1 The centre/place of calling off/withdrawing of the Non-Cooperation Movement   **[CBSE 2013]**

2 The place known for the movement of Indigo peasants during the British Period   **[CBSE 2020, 16]**

3 The place where Gandhiji started the Satyagraha in favour of cotton mill workers   **[CBSE 2013, 12]**

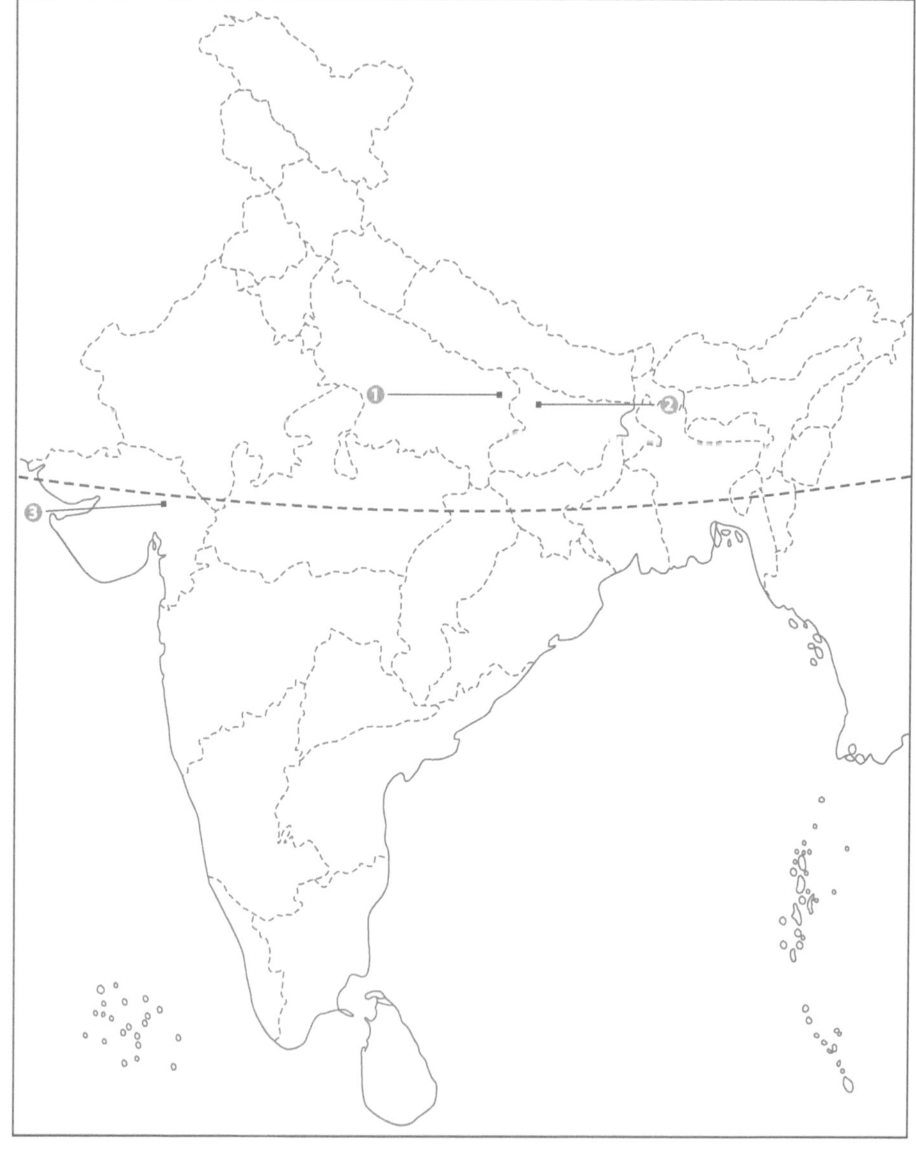

Practice Map 3

 On the given political map of India, name and locate the following.

1 The place where Gandhiji started the Satyagraha in support of the peasants of Gujarat in 1917   [CBSE 2012]

2 A place associated with Jallianwala Bagh Incident

3 The place from where Civil Disobedience Movement/ Salt Satyagraha was started   [CBSE 2012]

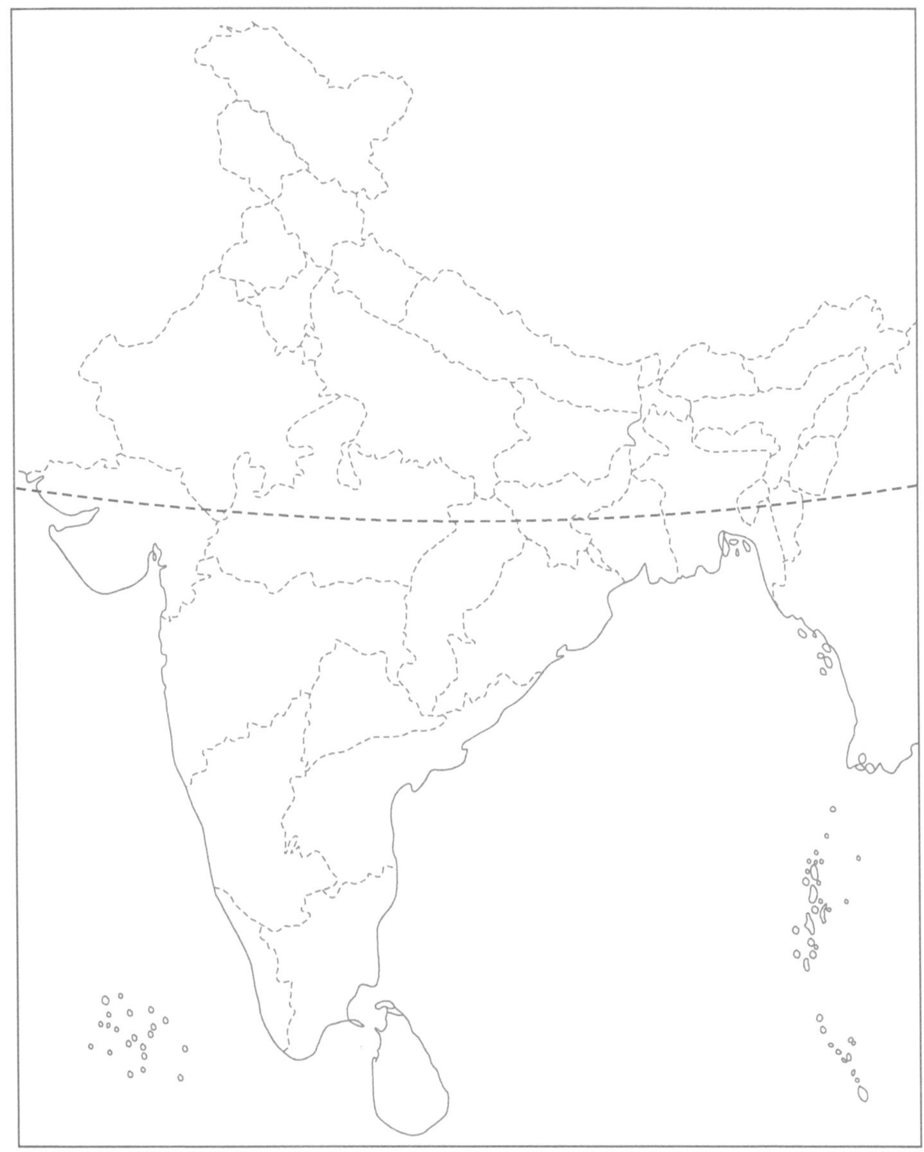

Exam Practice

Map 1

Q1 On the given political map of India, name and locate the following:

1. The place where the session of Indian National Congress was held in December 1920.
2. The place where Gandhiji started Satyagraha in favour of cotton mill workers.

Map 2

Q 2 Features are marked in the given political map of India. Identify these features with the help of the following information and write their correct names on the lines marked in the map.

1 The place where the Indian National Congress Session of September 1920 was held   [CBSE 2012]

2 The place where the Indian National Congress Session was held in 1927   [CBSE 2016]

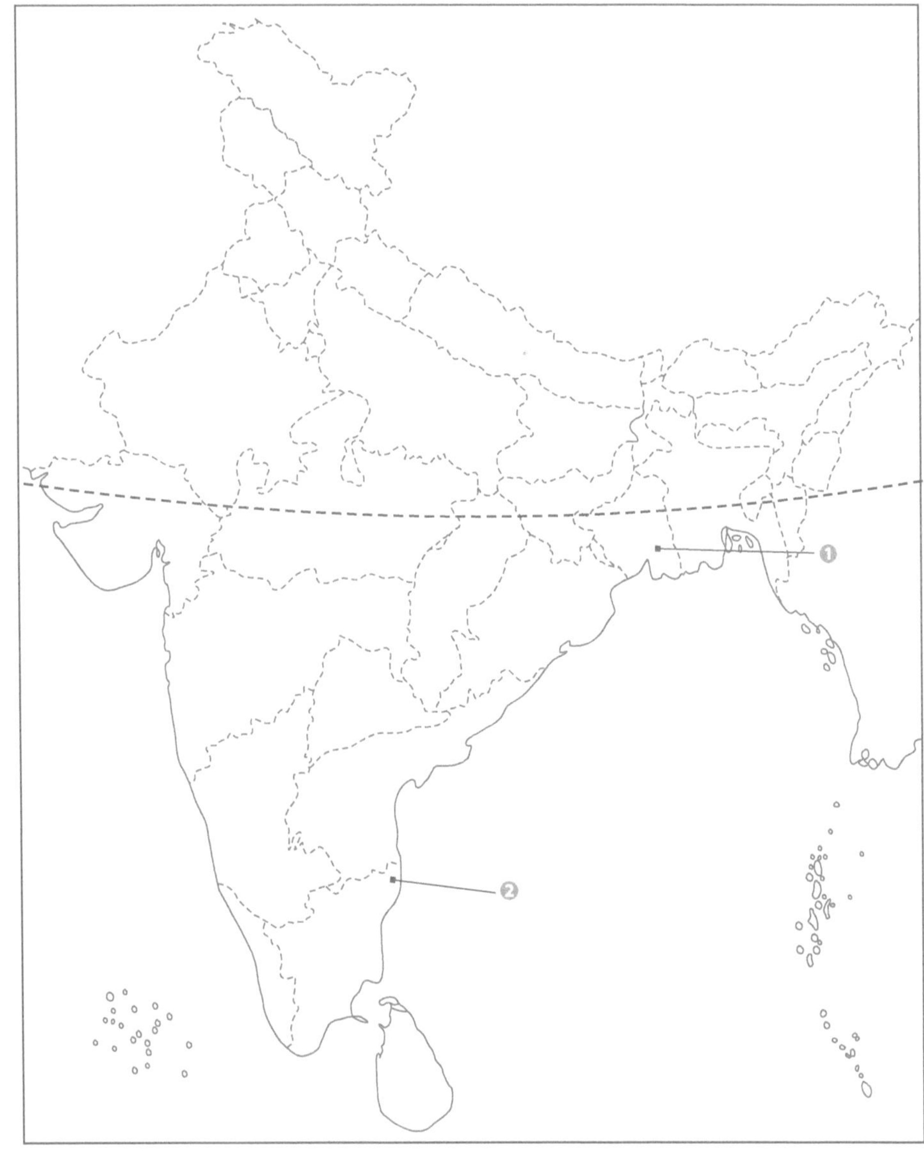

Answers (Practice Map)

Map 1

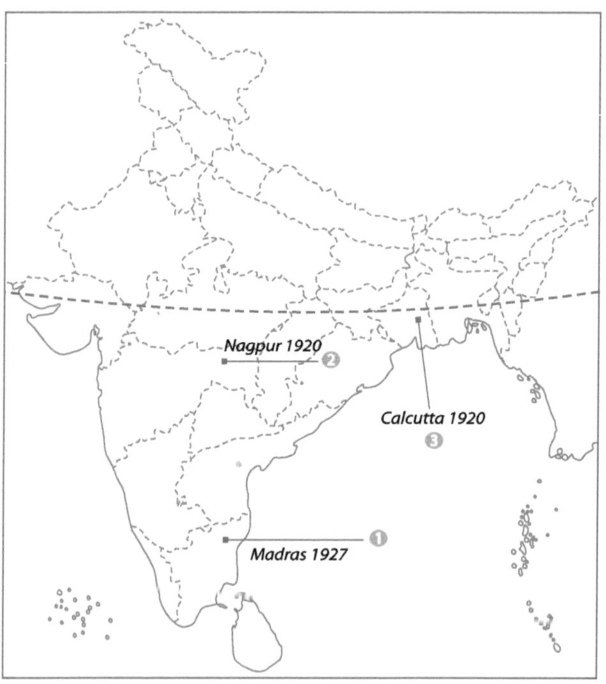

Map 2

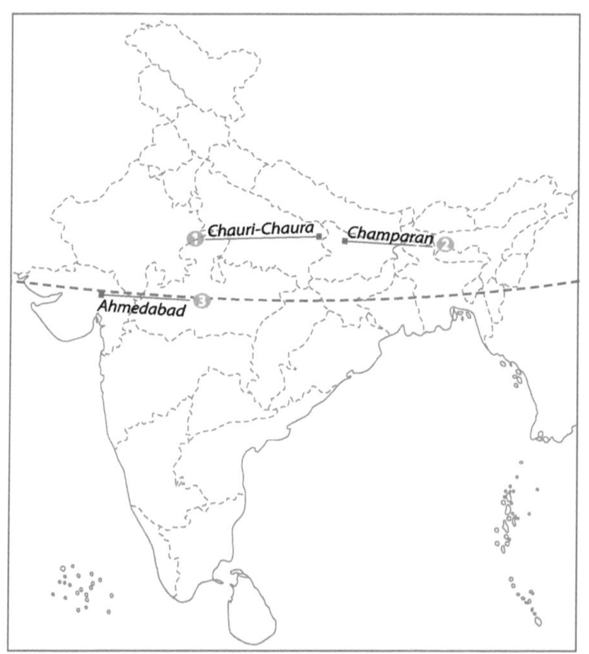

Map 3

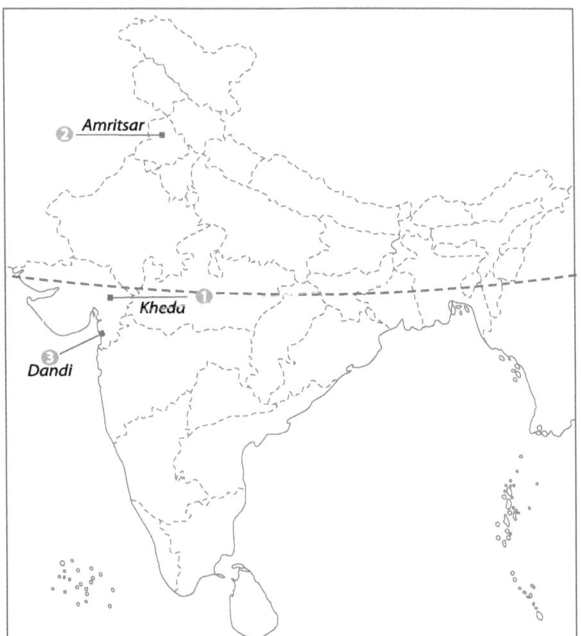

Answers (Exam Practice)

Map 1

Map 2

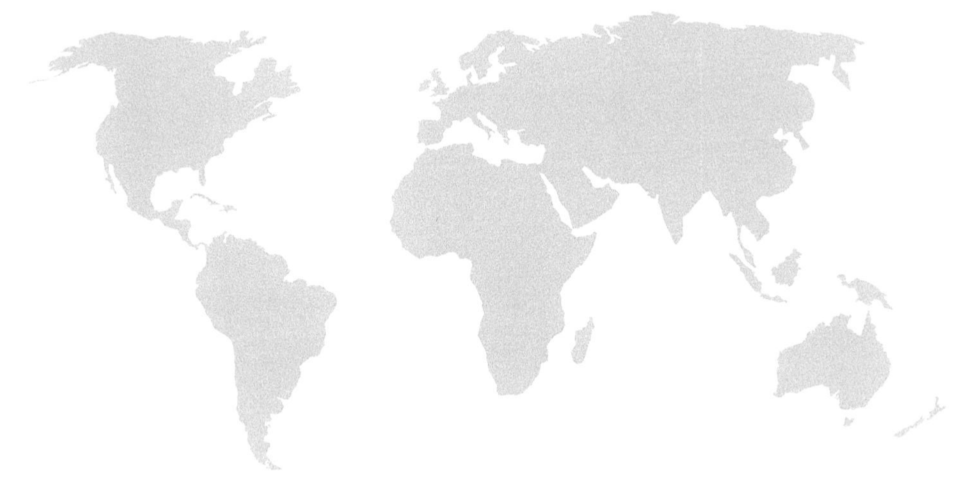

GEOGRAPHY

INDIA : Resource and Development
(Chapter-1 Resource and Development)

Six different types of soils are found in India. These are : Alluvial soil, Red soil, Black soil, Laterite soil, Mountain soil and Desert soil or Arid soil. Soils in India differ in composition and structure. This map shows the major soil types of India.

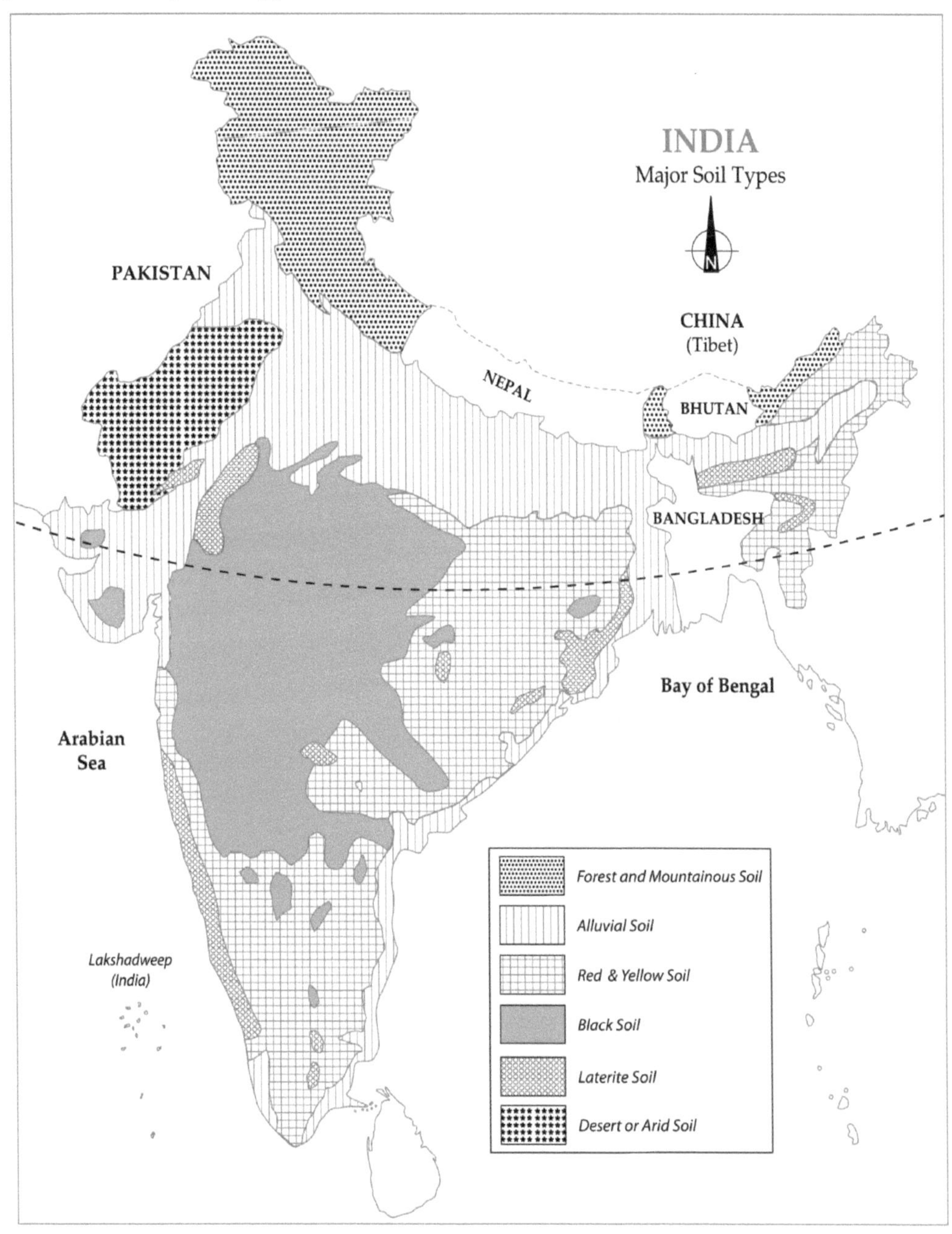

Practice Map 1

Q1 Features are marked by numbers in the given outline map of India. Identify these features with the help of following information and write their correct names on the lines marked in the map.

1 A major soil type [CBSE 2012, 11, 10]

2 Soil type that are formed where the rainfall is low [CBSE 2012, 10]

3 Soil type found mainly in hill slopes [CBSE 2012, 11]

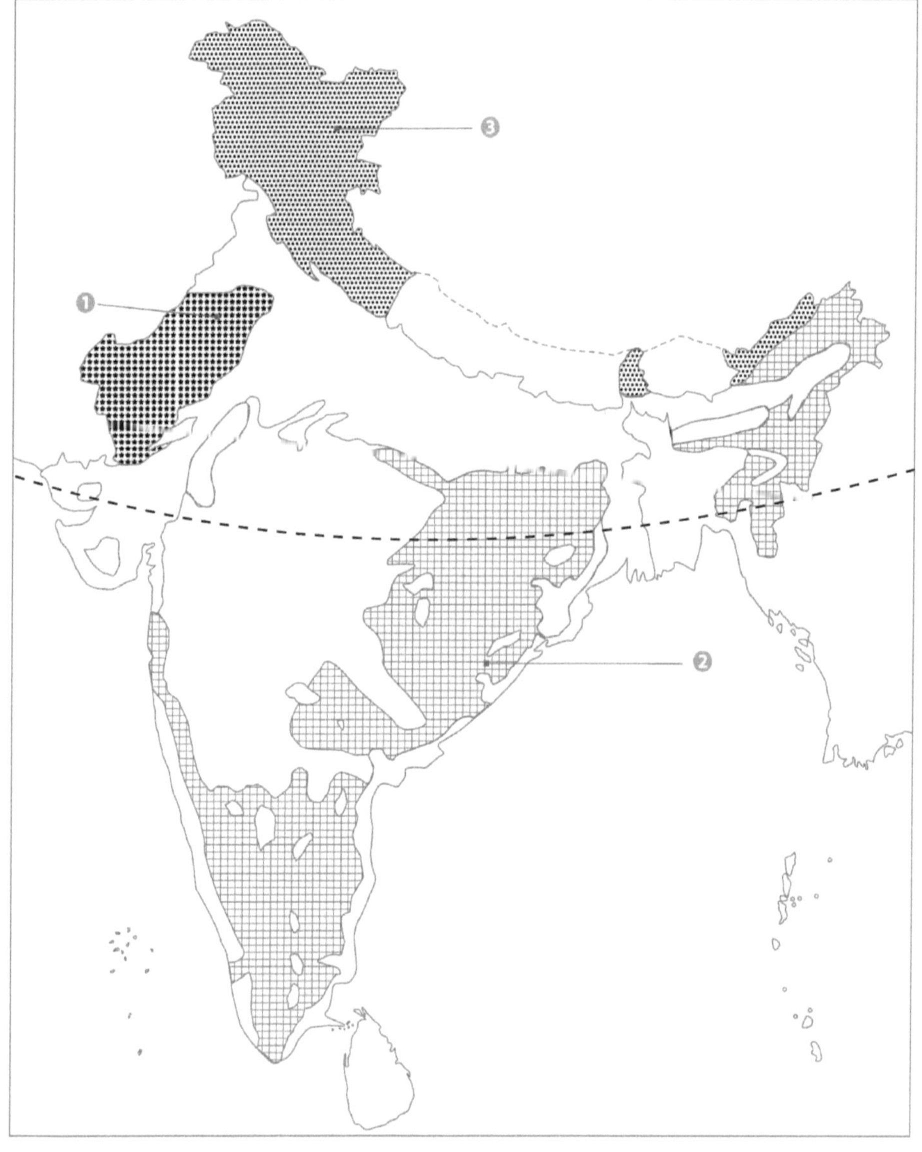

INDIA : Major Dams and Rivers of India
(Chapter-3 Water Resources)

This map shows the major dams and rivers of India. A dam is a structure, designed to hold back water in a lake, river, stream or other water body.

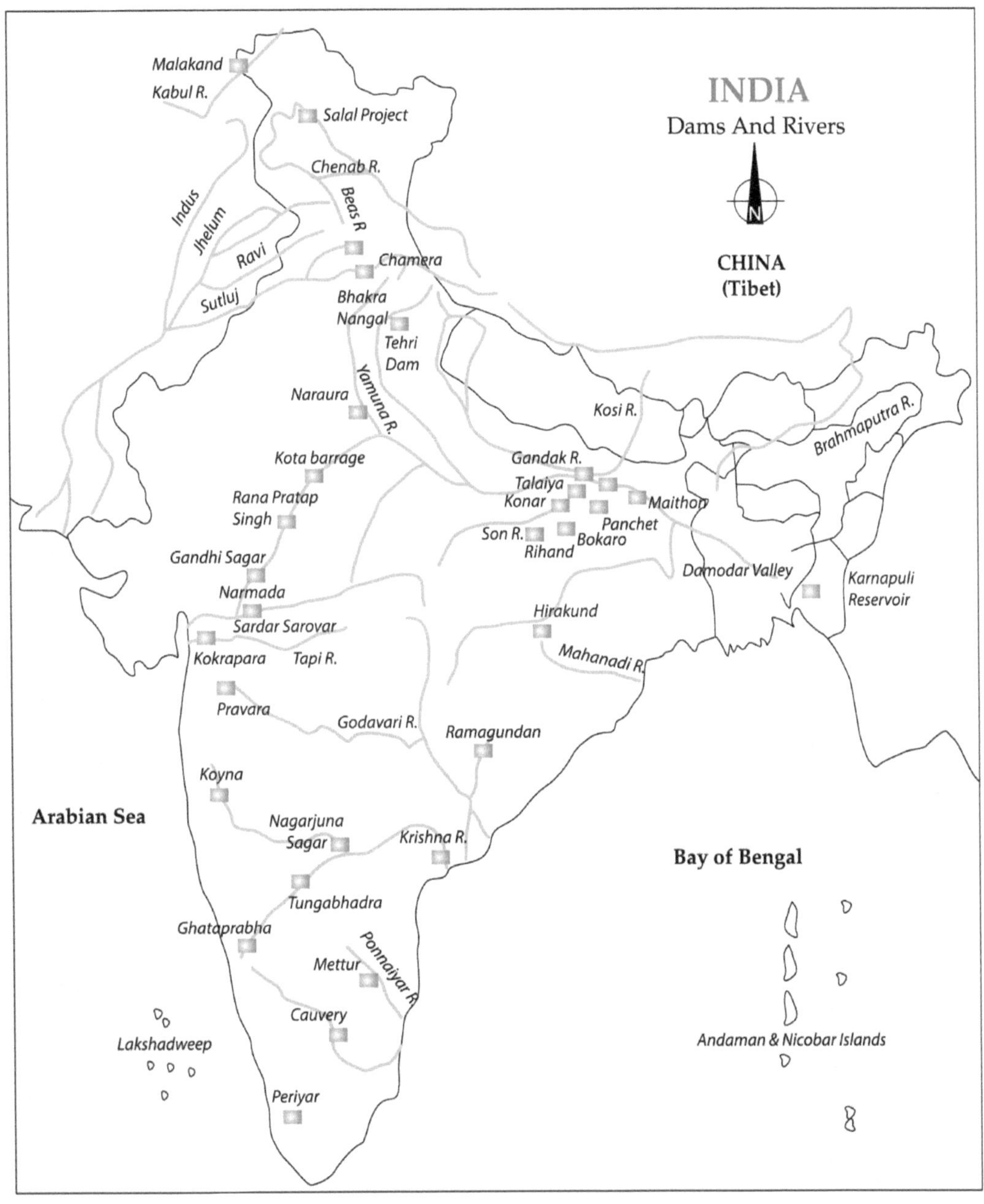

Practice Map 2

Q2 Locate and label the following items on the given map with appropriate symbols.

1 Tehri dam	[CBSE 2012, 11, 10]
2 Bhakra Nangal dam
3 Rana Pratap Sagar dam	[CBSE 2012, 11, 10]
4 Salal dam	[CBSE 2012, 11]

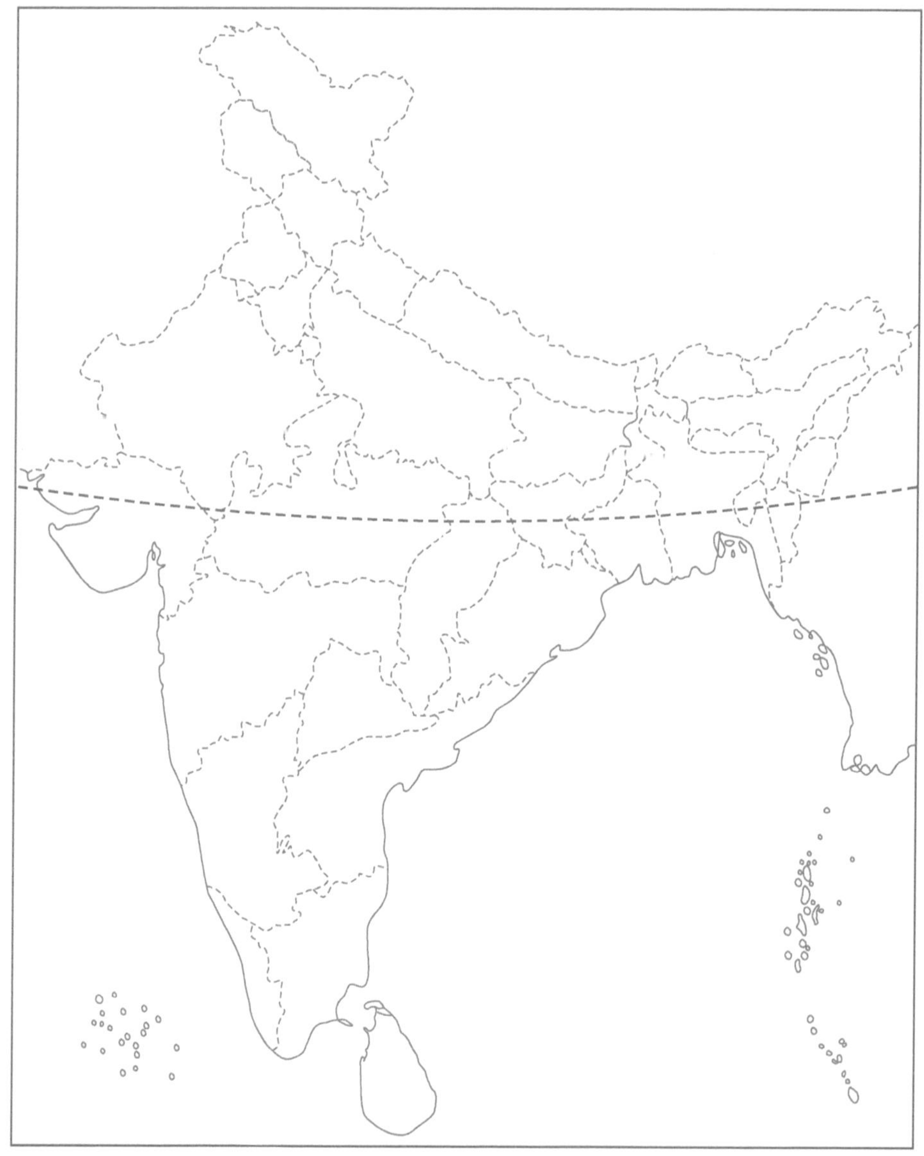

Practice Map 3

Q3 Locate and label the following items on the given map with appropriate symbols.

1. Tungabhadra dam
2. Nagarjuna Sagar dam
3. Hirakud dam
4. Sardar Sarovar dam

[CBSE 2020]

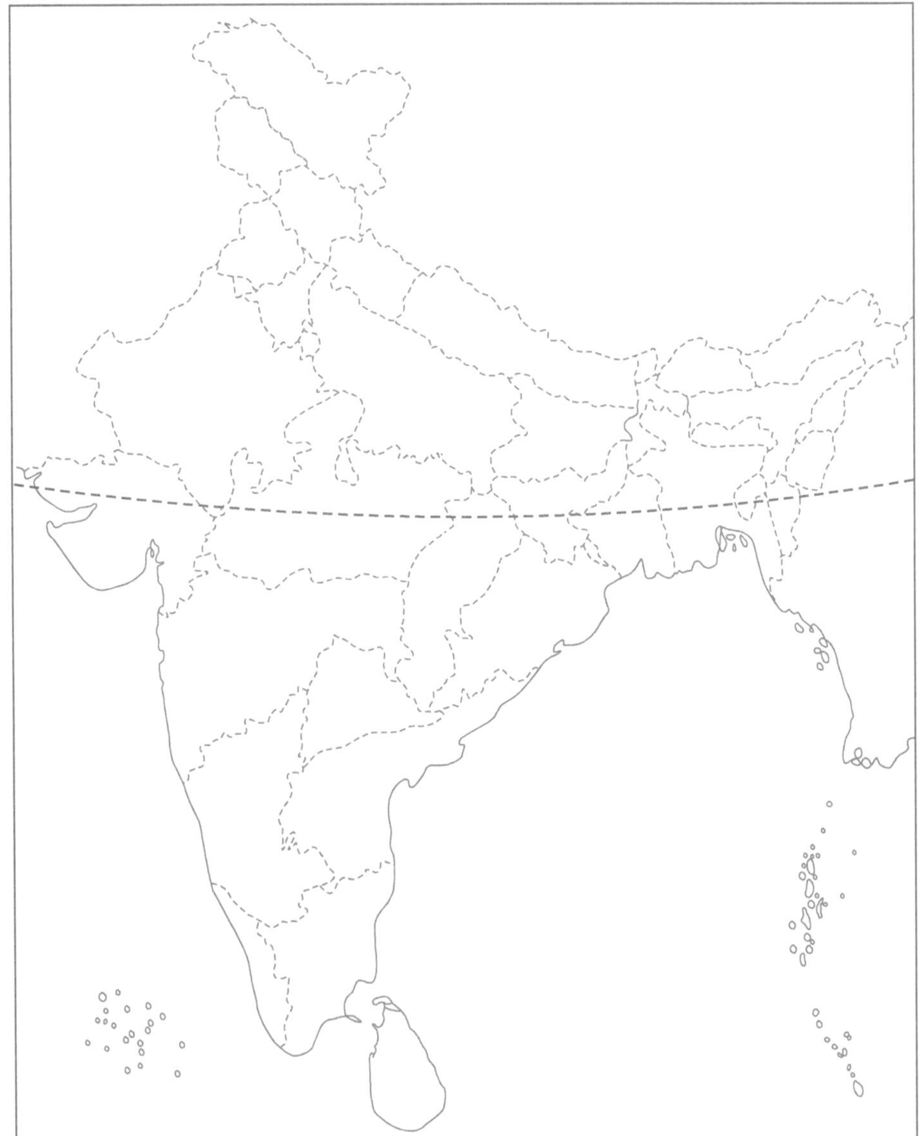

Wheat Growing Areas of India
(Chapter-4 Agriculture)

Uttar Pradesh is the largest producer of wheat, accounting for over 34 per cent of the wheat produced in India. This map shows the wheat growing areas of India.

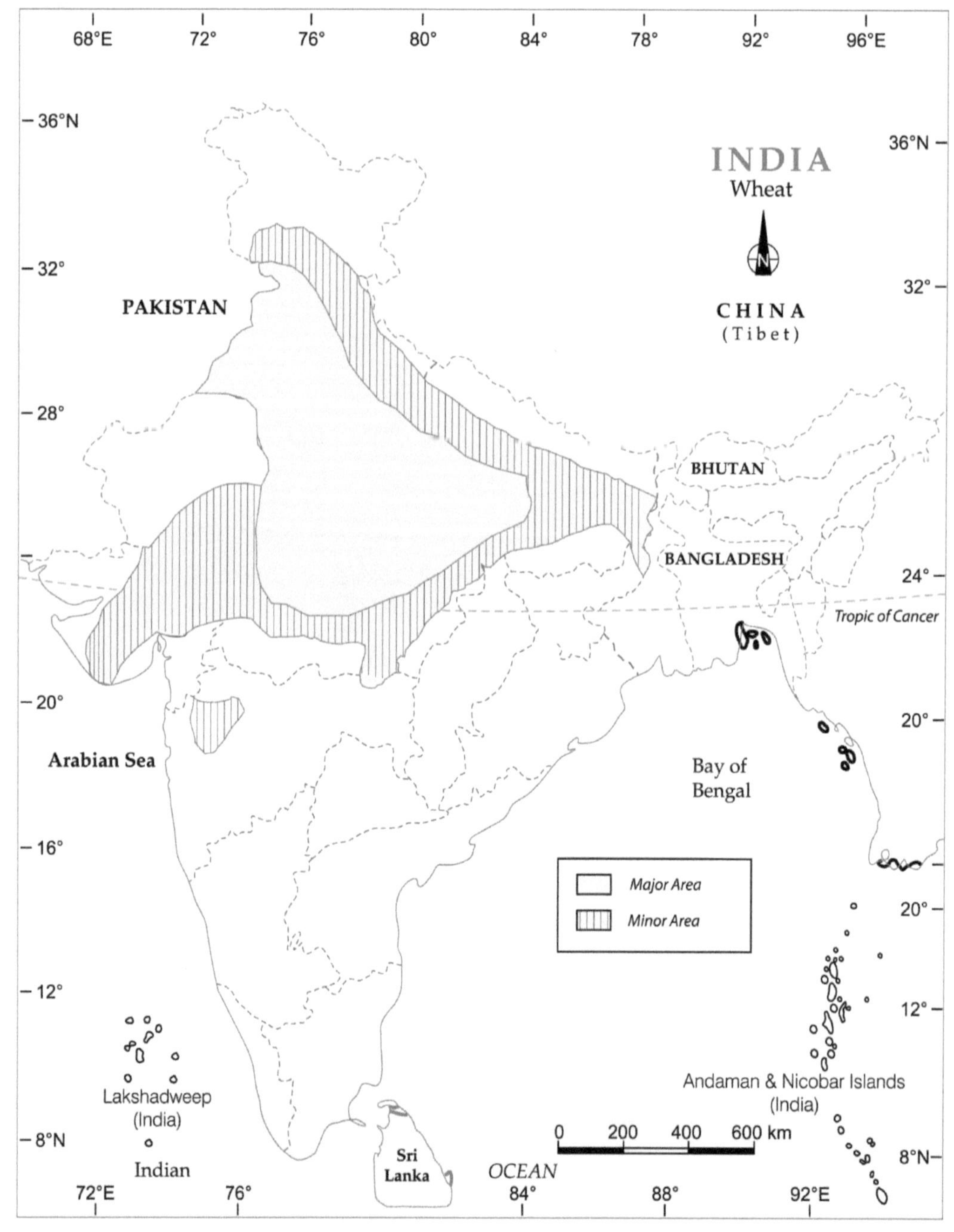

Practice Map 4

Q 4 On the given political map of India, four leading wheat growing states of India are marked by 1, 2, 3 and 4. Identify these and write their correct names on the line drawn against each in the given map.

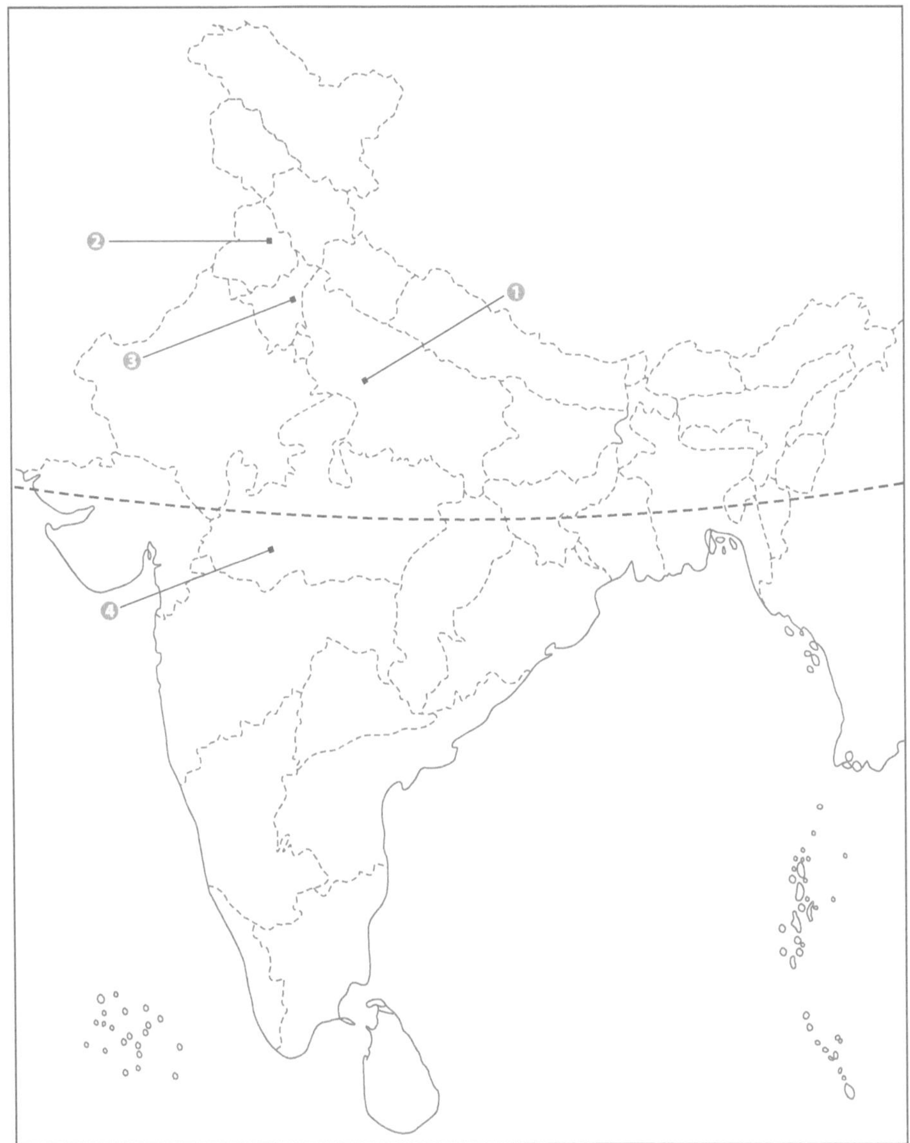

Rice Growing Areas of India
(Chapter-4 Agriculture)

Among the rice producing states, West Bengal is the most important producer and ranks at the leading position, accounting for about 15 per cent of the total quantity of rice produced in India. This map shows the rice growing areas of India.

Practice Map 5

Q5 On the given political map of India, four leading rice growing states of India are marked by 1, 2, 3 and 4. Identify these and write their correct names on the line drawn against each in the given map.

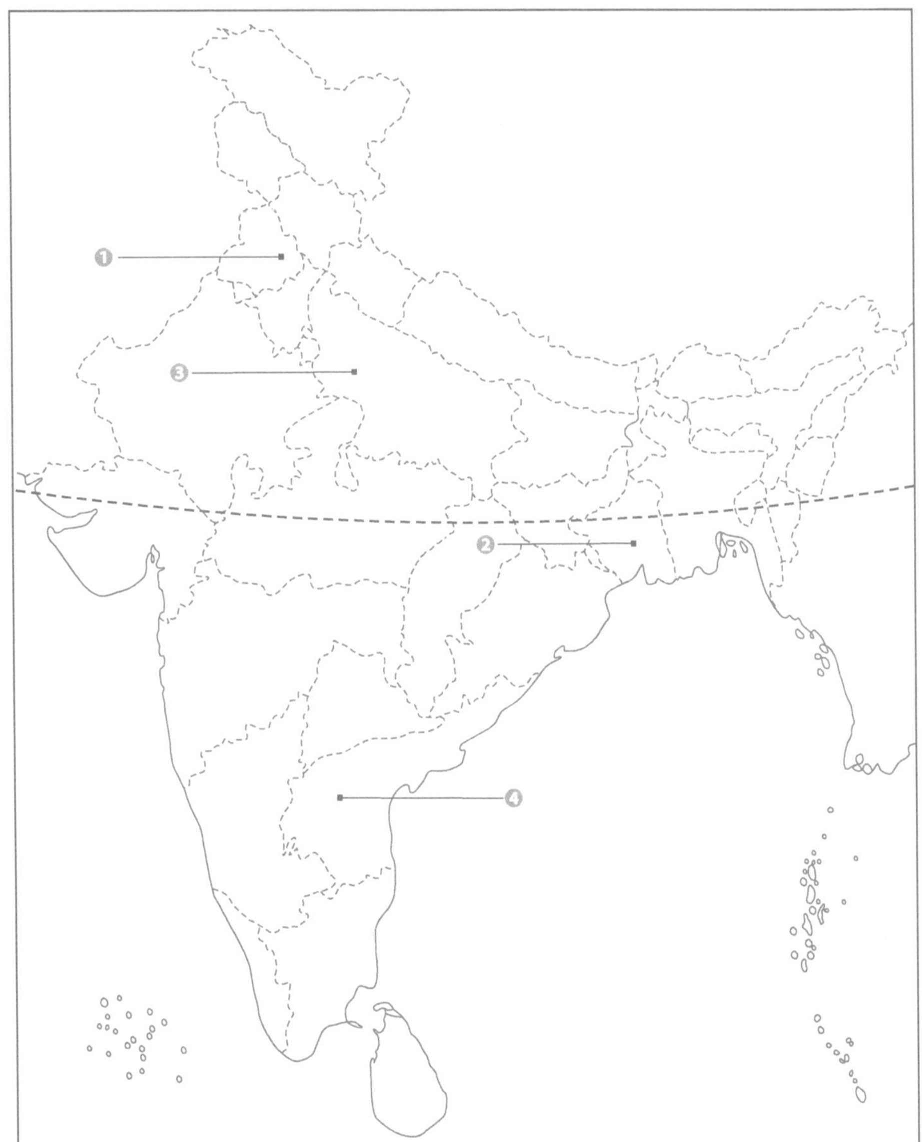

Sugarcane Growing Areas of India
(Chapter-4 Agriculture)

This map shows the sugarcane growing areas of India.

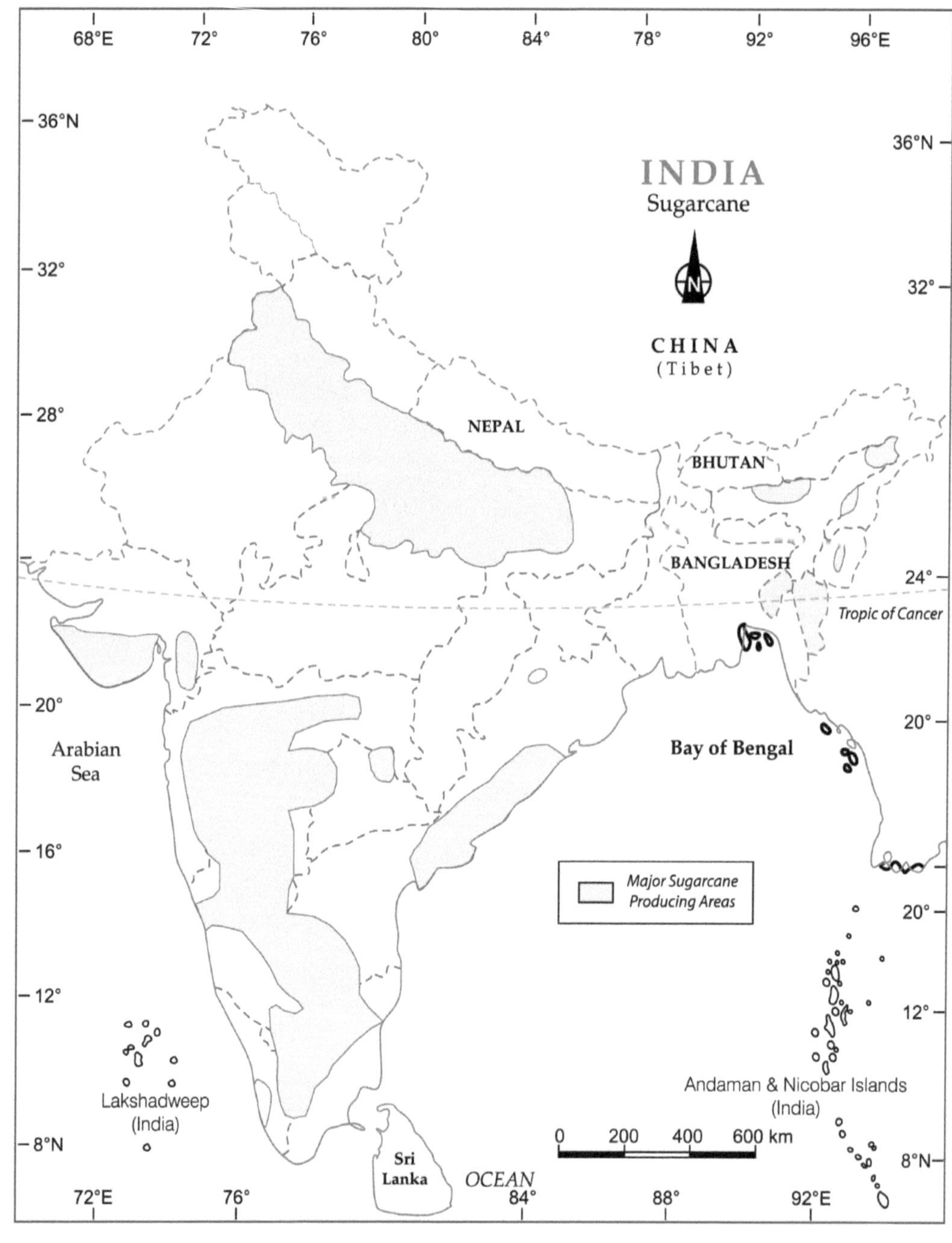

Practice Map 6

Q6 On the given political map of India, three leading sugarcane growing states of India are marked by 1, 2 and 3. Identify these and write their correct names on the line drawn against each in the given map.

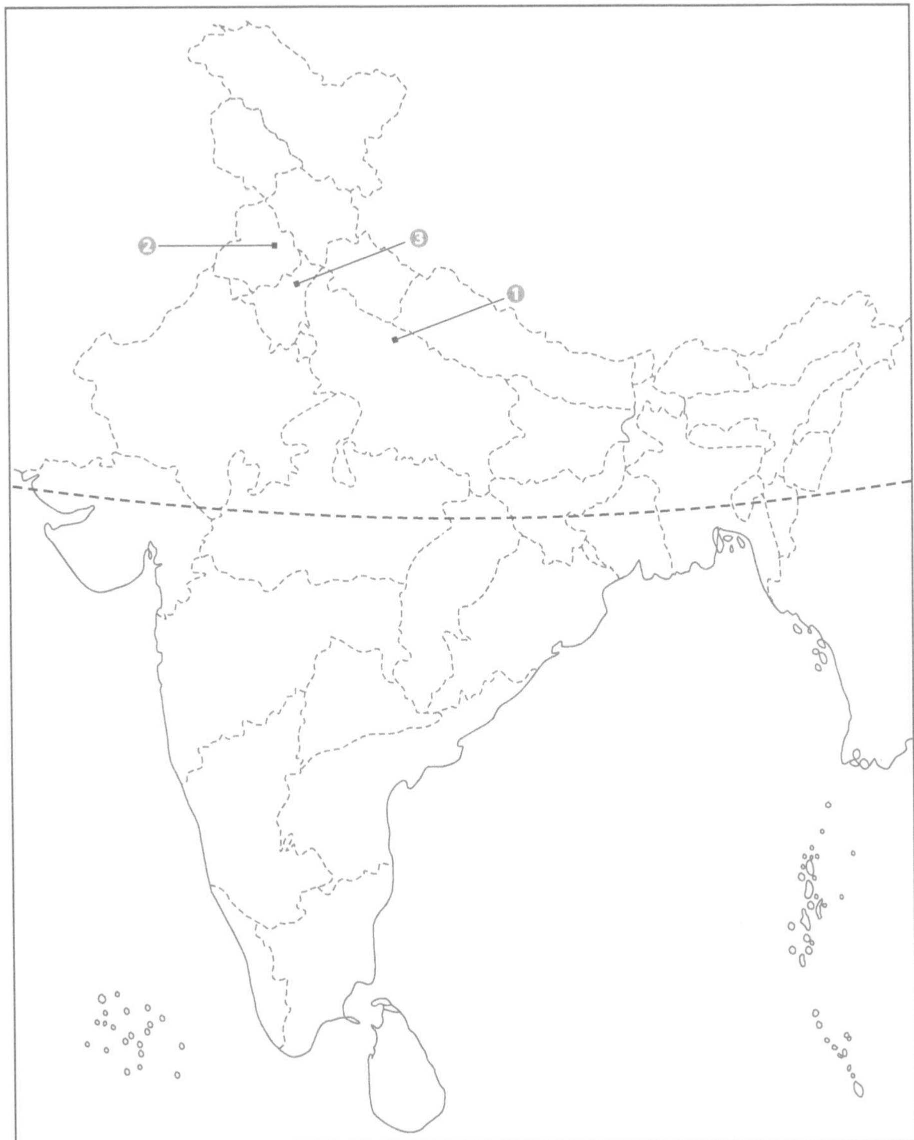

Tea and Coffee Producing Areas of India
(Chapter-4 Agriculture)

Assam is the largest producer of tea and accounts for more than 52 per cent of the tea produced in India. Karnataka is the largest producer of coffee and accounts for more than 53 per cent of the coffee produced in India. This map shows the tea and coffee producing areas of India.

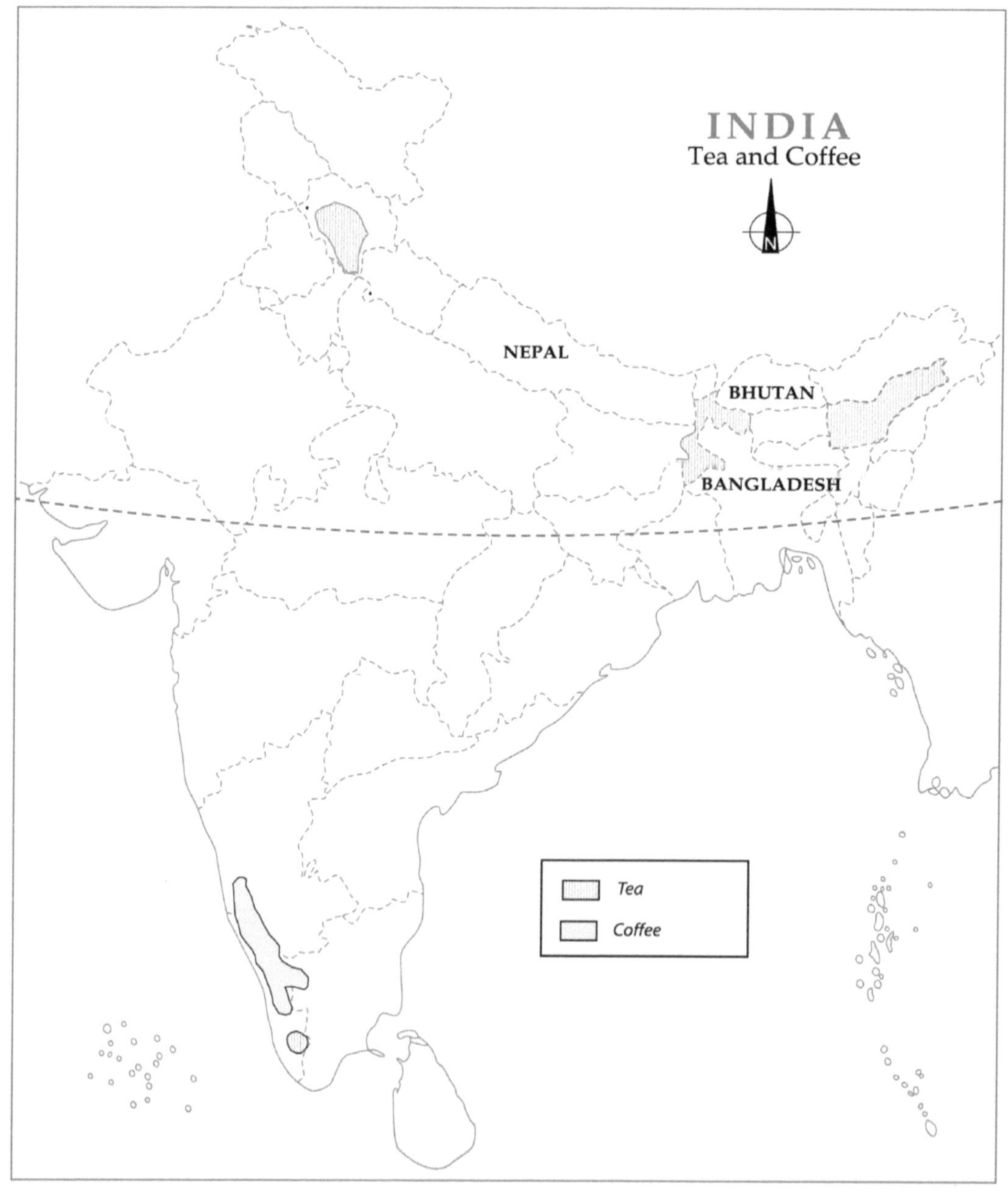

Practice Map 7

Q7 On the given political map of India two items are marked as 1 and 2. Identify these and write their correct names.

1 Largest producer of tea
2 Largest producer of coffee

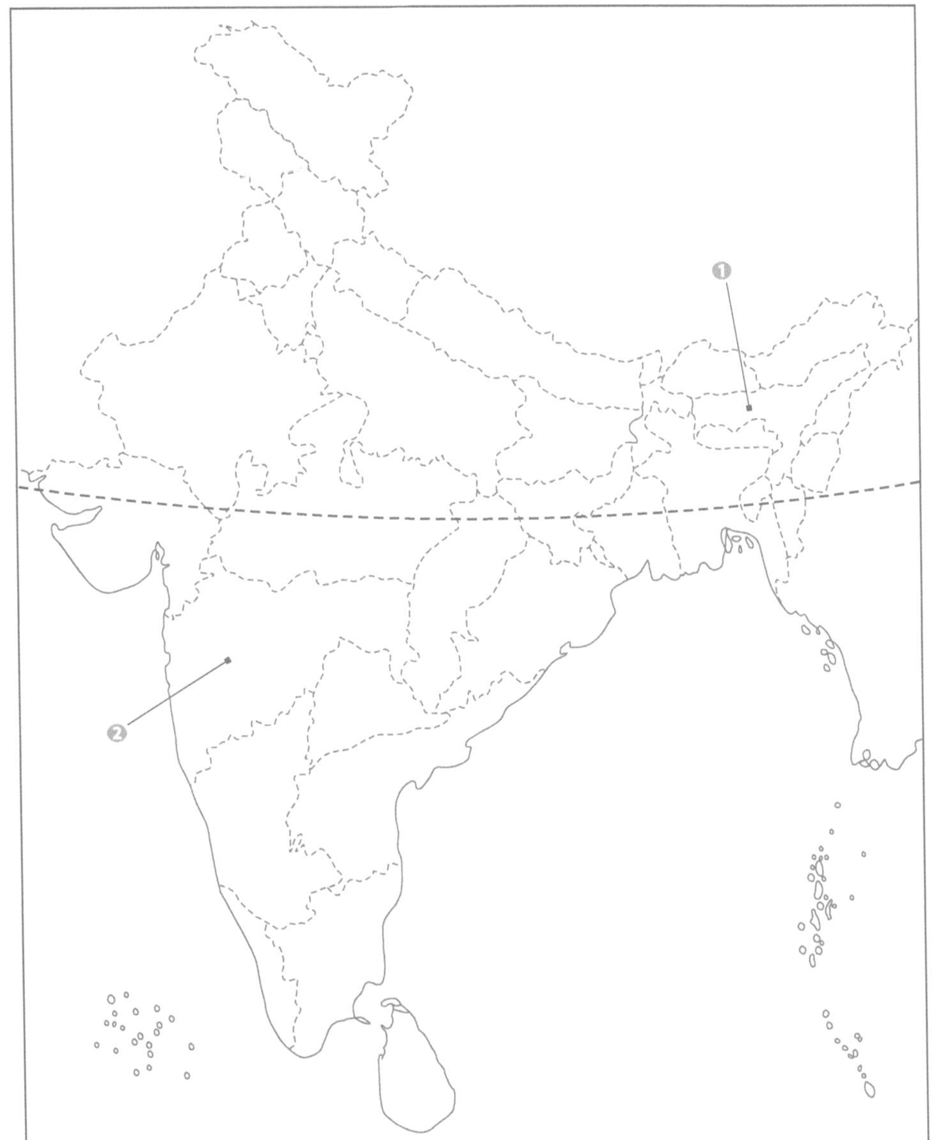

Jute and Rubber Producing Areas of India
(Chapter-4 Agriculture)

West Bengal is the largest producer of jute, while Kerala is the largest producer of rubber in India. This map shows the jute and rubber producing regions of India.

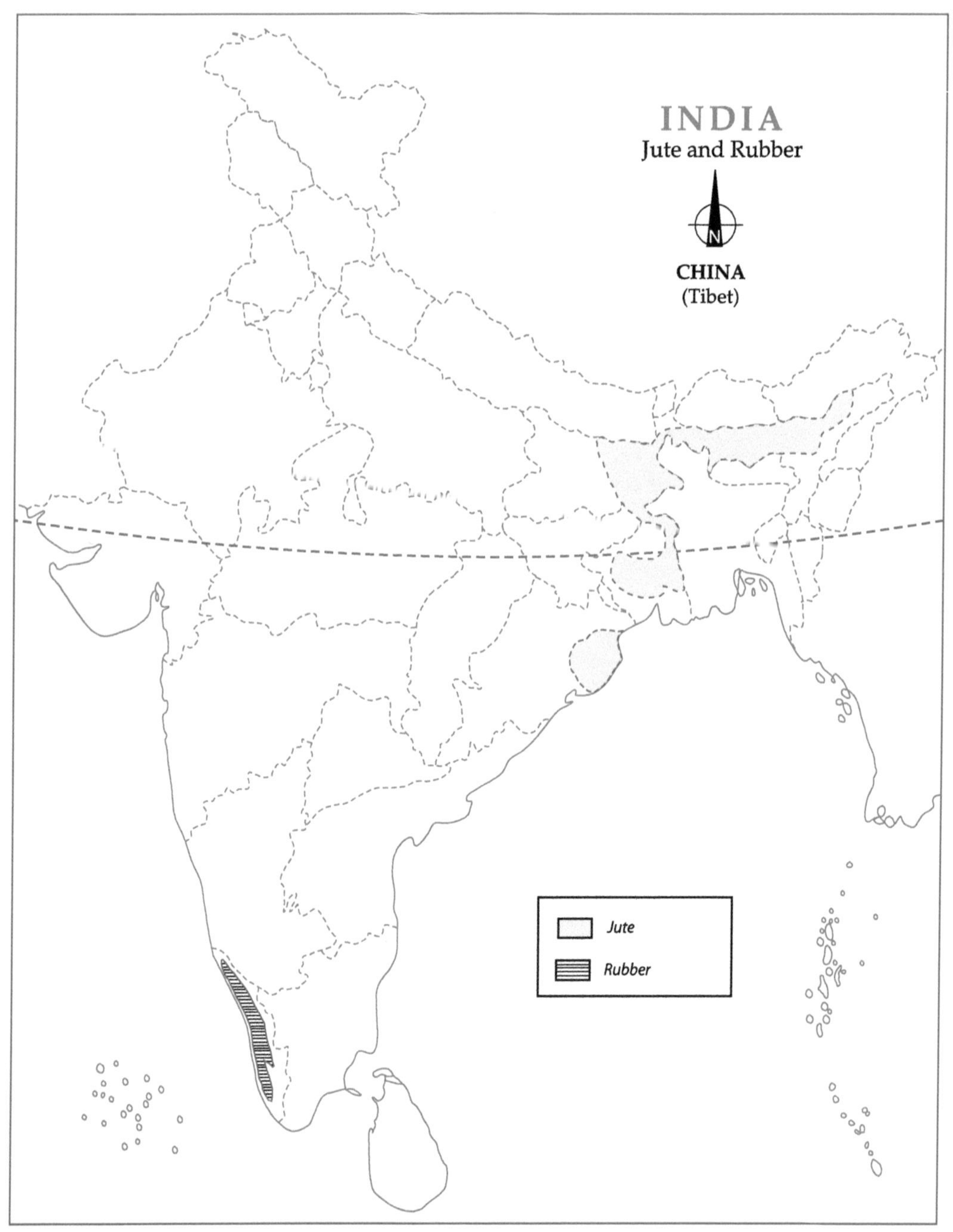

Practice Map 8

Q 8 On the given political map of India two items as 1 and 2. Identify these and write their correct names.

   1 Largest producer of Jute

   2 Largest producer of Rubber

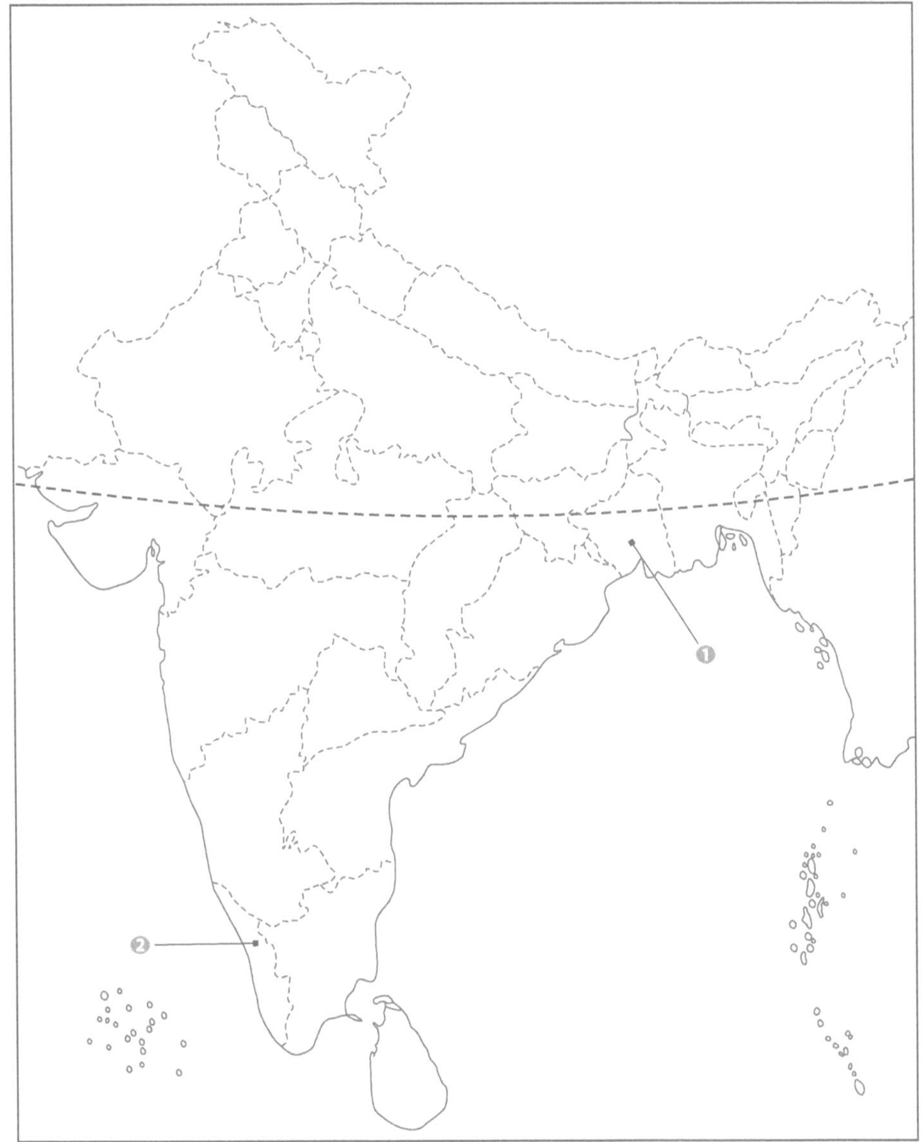

Cotton Producing Areas of India
(Chapter-4 Agriculture)

This map shows the cotton producing regions of India. Gujarat is the largest producer of cotton in India.

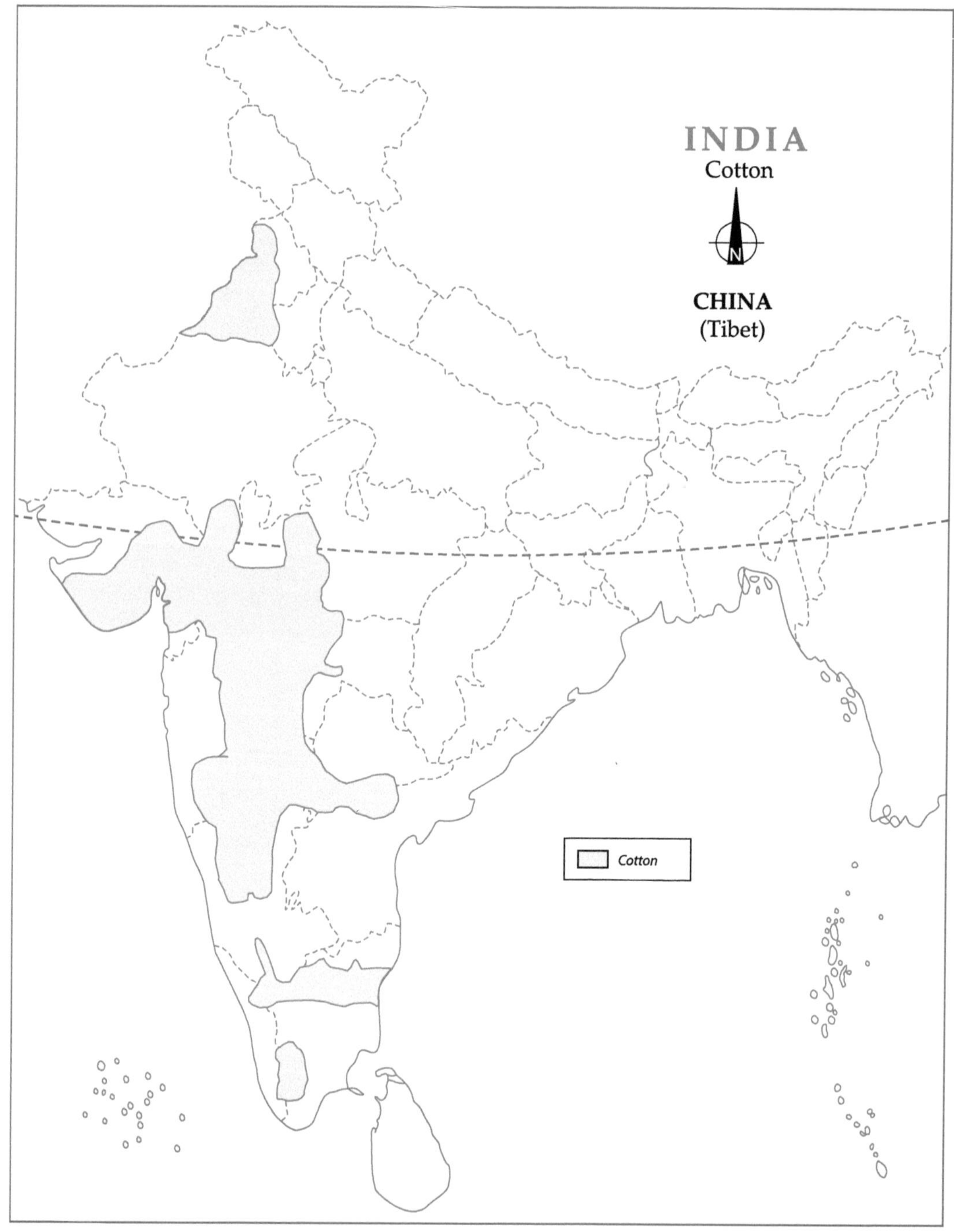

Q9 On the given outline map of India two leading producers of cotton are marked as 1 and 2. Identify these and write their correct names.

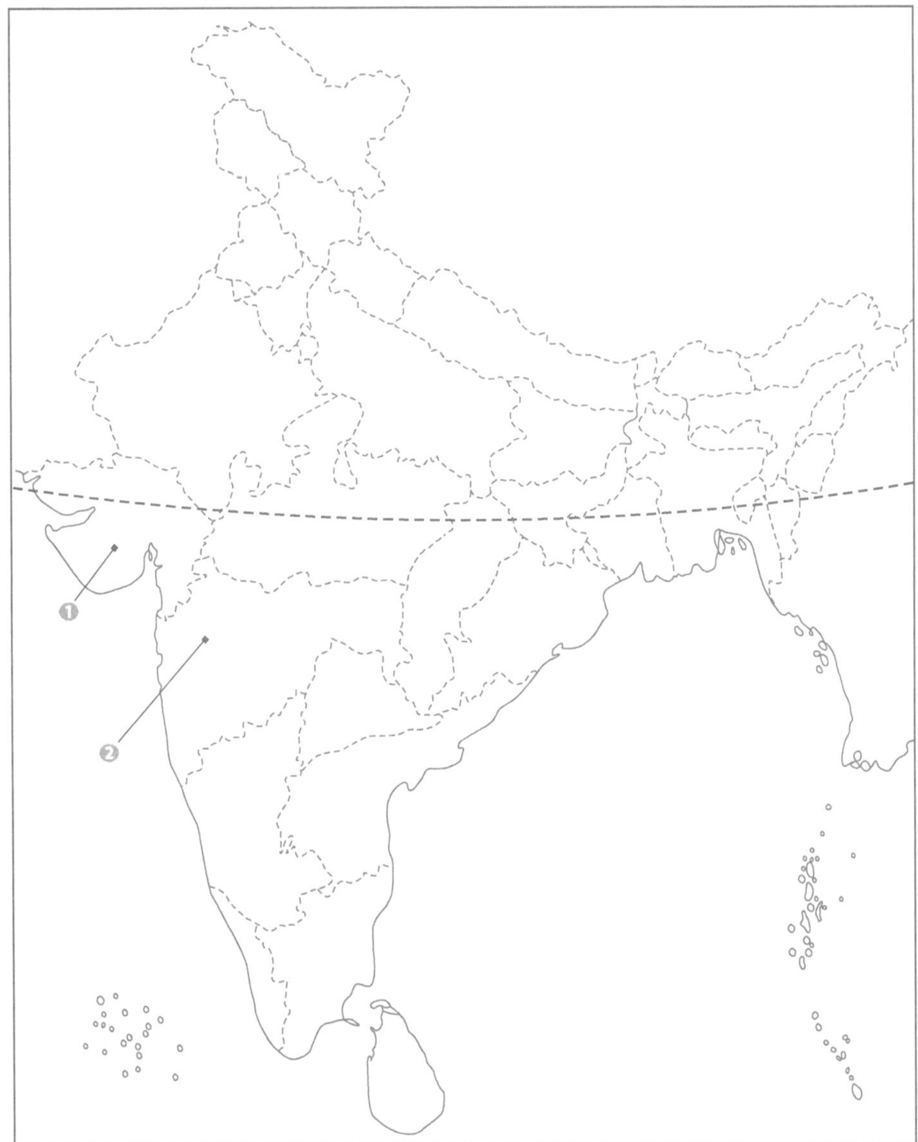

INDIA : Coal Mines and Oil Fields of India
(Chapter-5 Minerals and Energy Resources)

This map shows the major coal mines and oil fields of India.

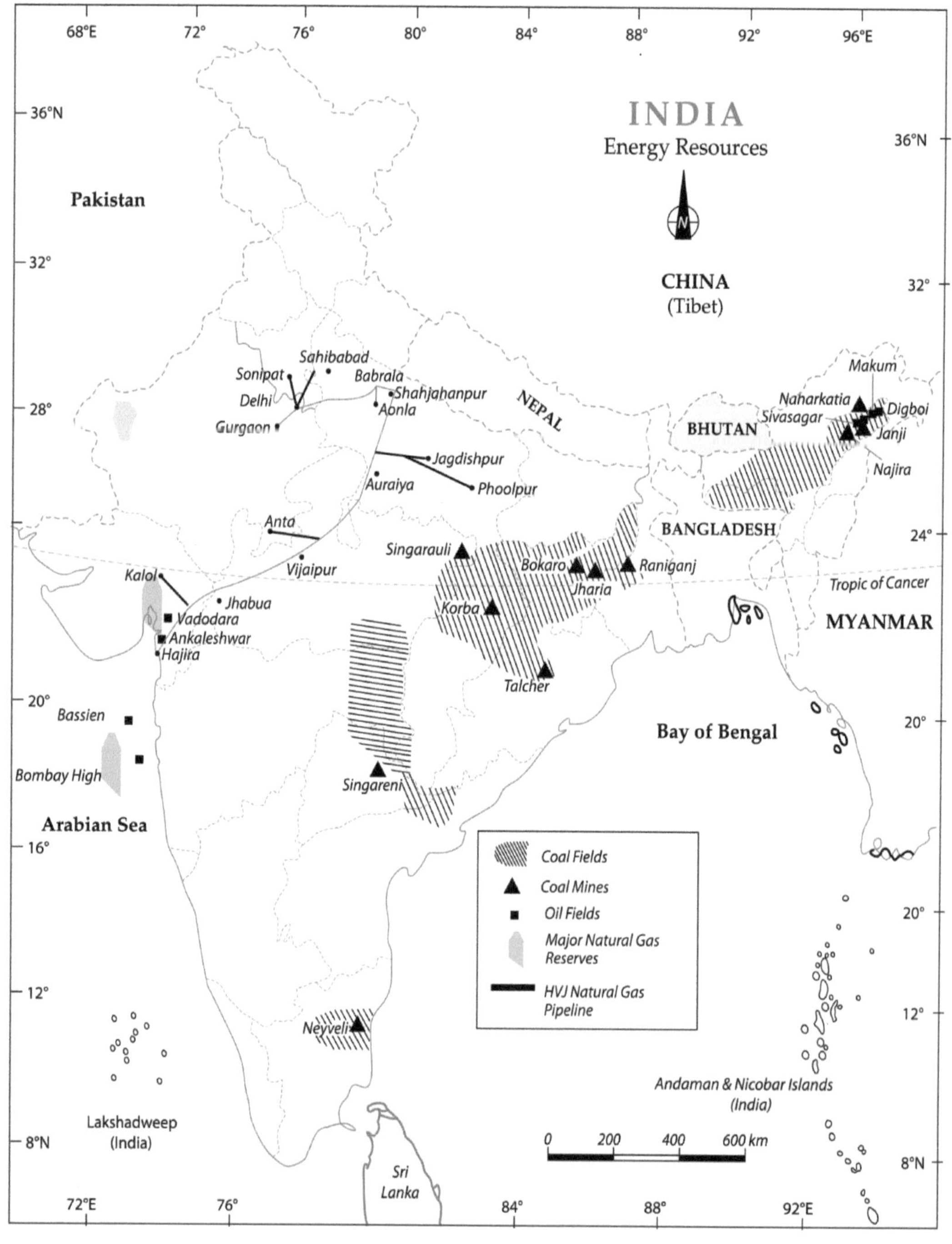

Practice Map 10

Q1 On the given political map of India four coal mines are marked as 1, 2, 3 and 4. Identify these and write their correct names.

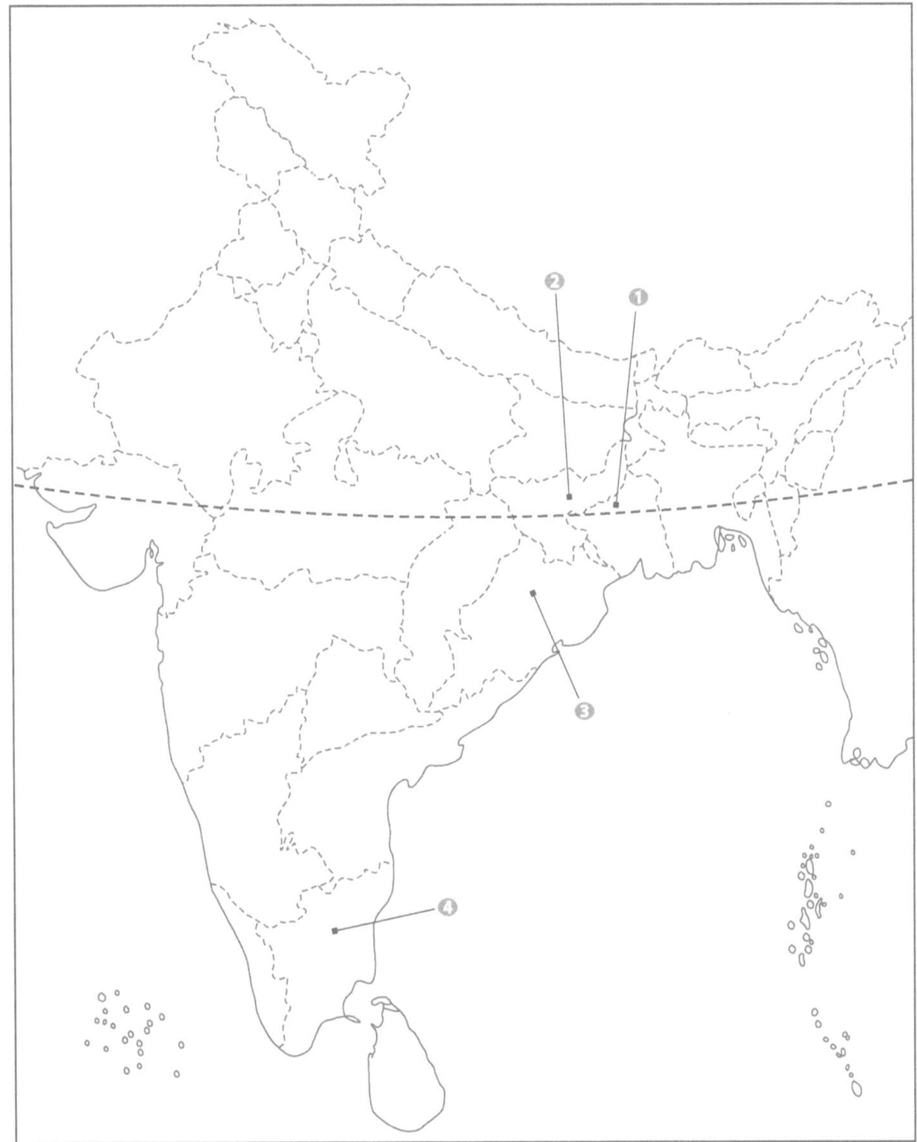

Practice Map 11

Q 11 On the given political map of India six oil fields are marked as 1, 2, 3, 4, 5 and 6. Identify these and write their correct names.

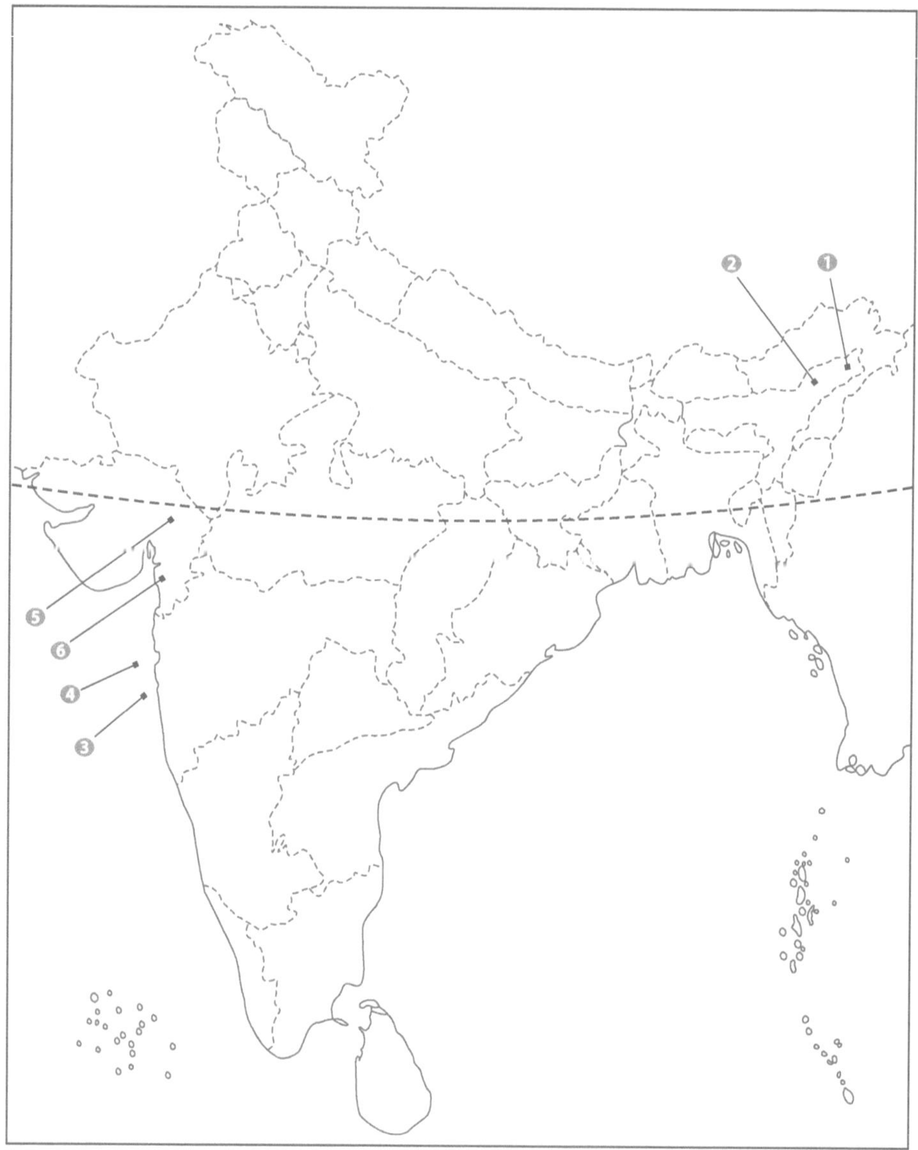

INDIA : Minerals
(Chapter-5 Minerals and Energy Resources)

This map shows the distribution of iron ore, manganese, bauxite and mica in India.

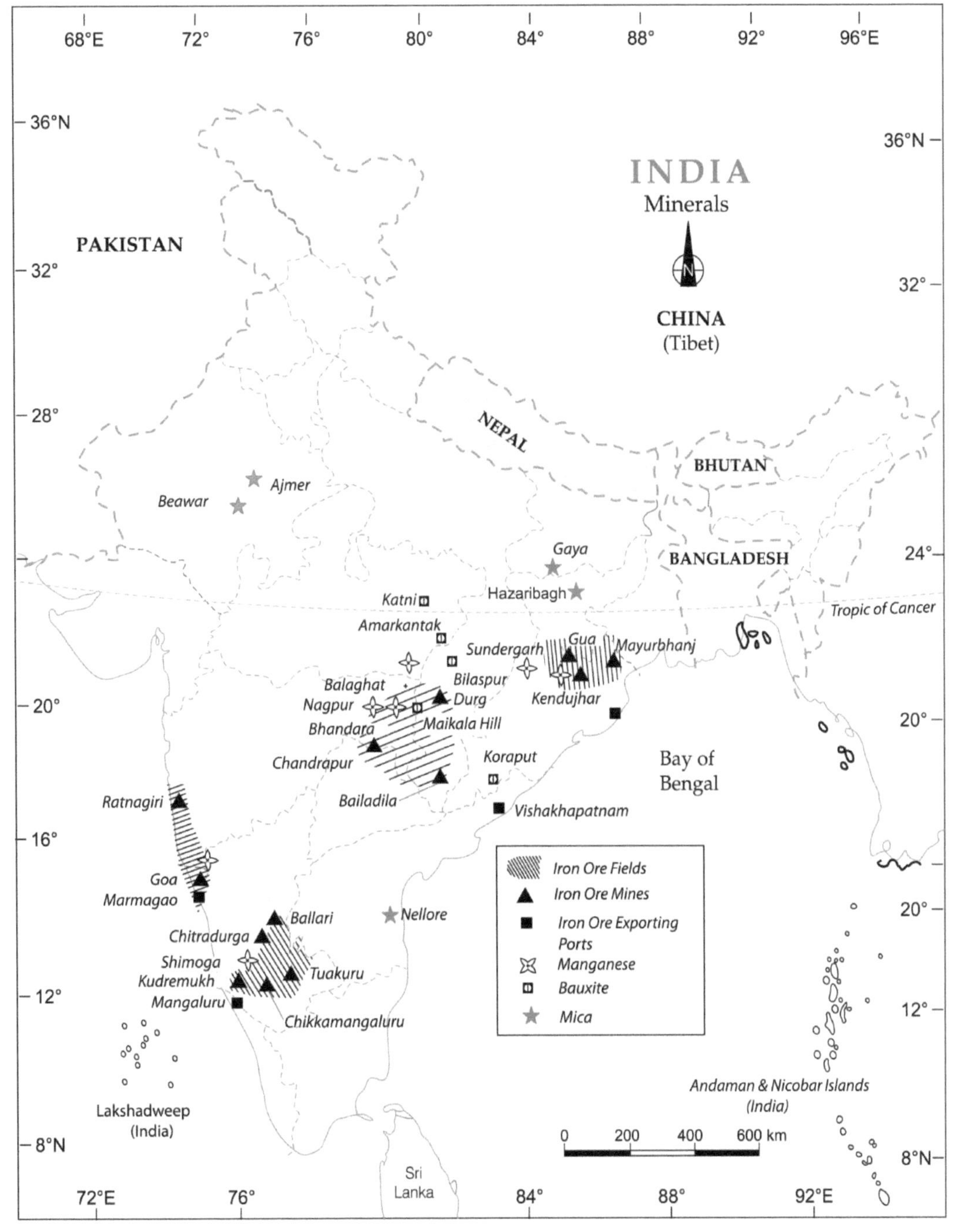

Practice Map 12

 On the given political map of India five iron ore mines are marked as 1, 2, 3, 4 and 5. Identify these and write their correct names.

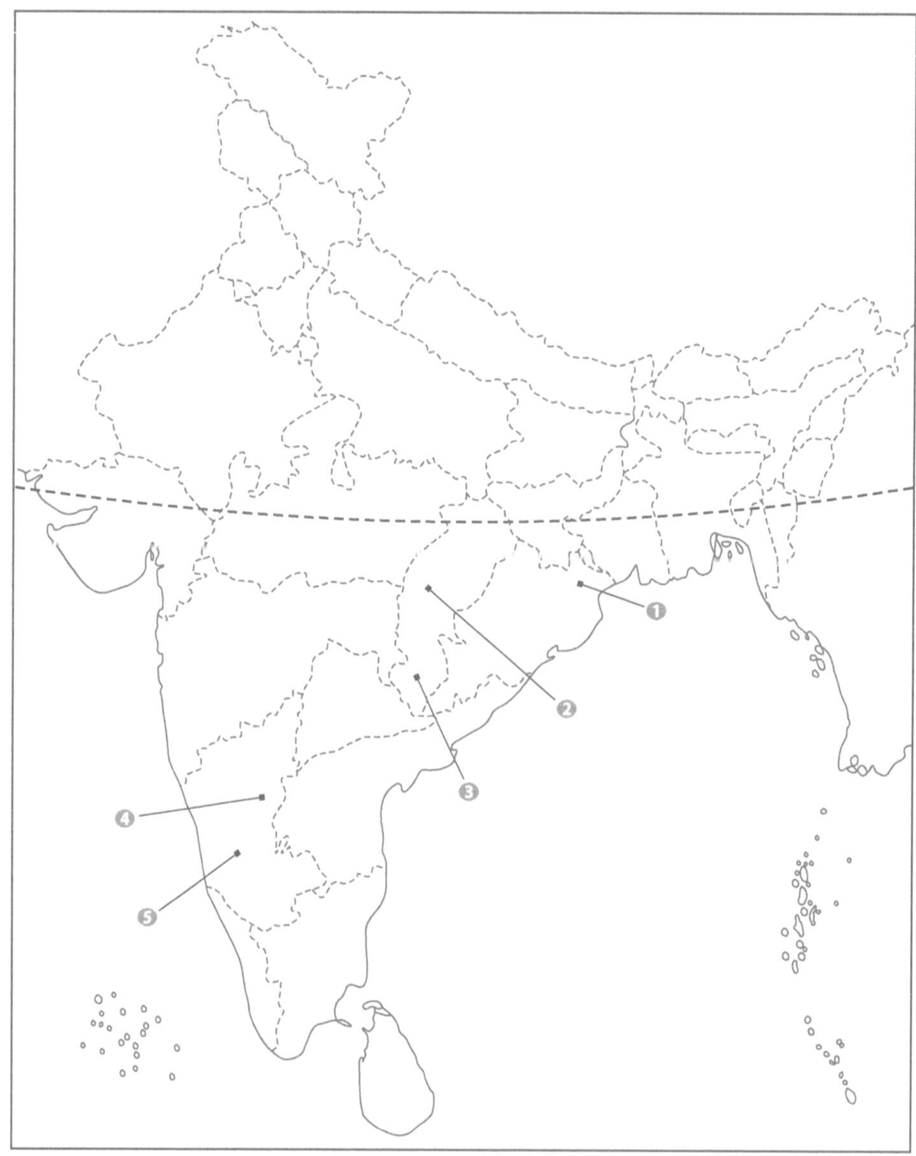

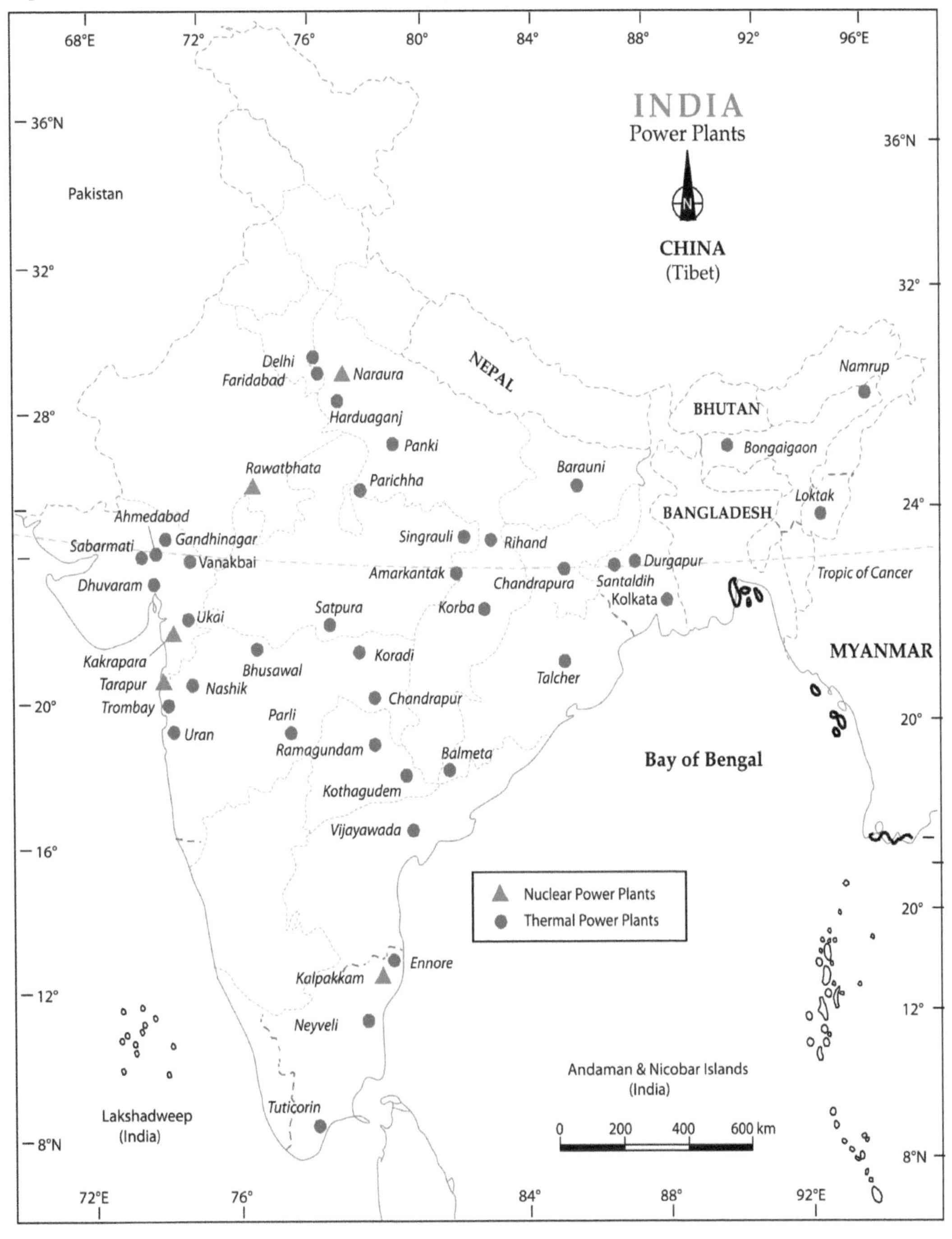

INDIA : Nuclear and Thermal Power Plants of India
(Chapter-5 Minerals and Energy Resources)

This map shows the nuclear and thermal power plants of India.

Practice Map 13

Q13 Locate and label the following items on the given map with appropriate symbols.

1 Naraura nuclear power plant   [CBSE 2020]

2 Kalpakkam nuclear power plant

3 Tarapur nuclear power plant   [CBSE 2016]

4 Kakrapara nuclear power plant

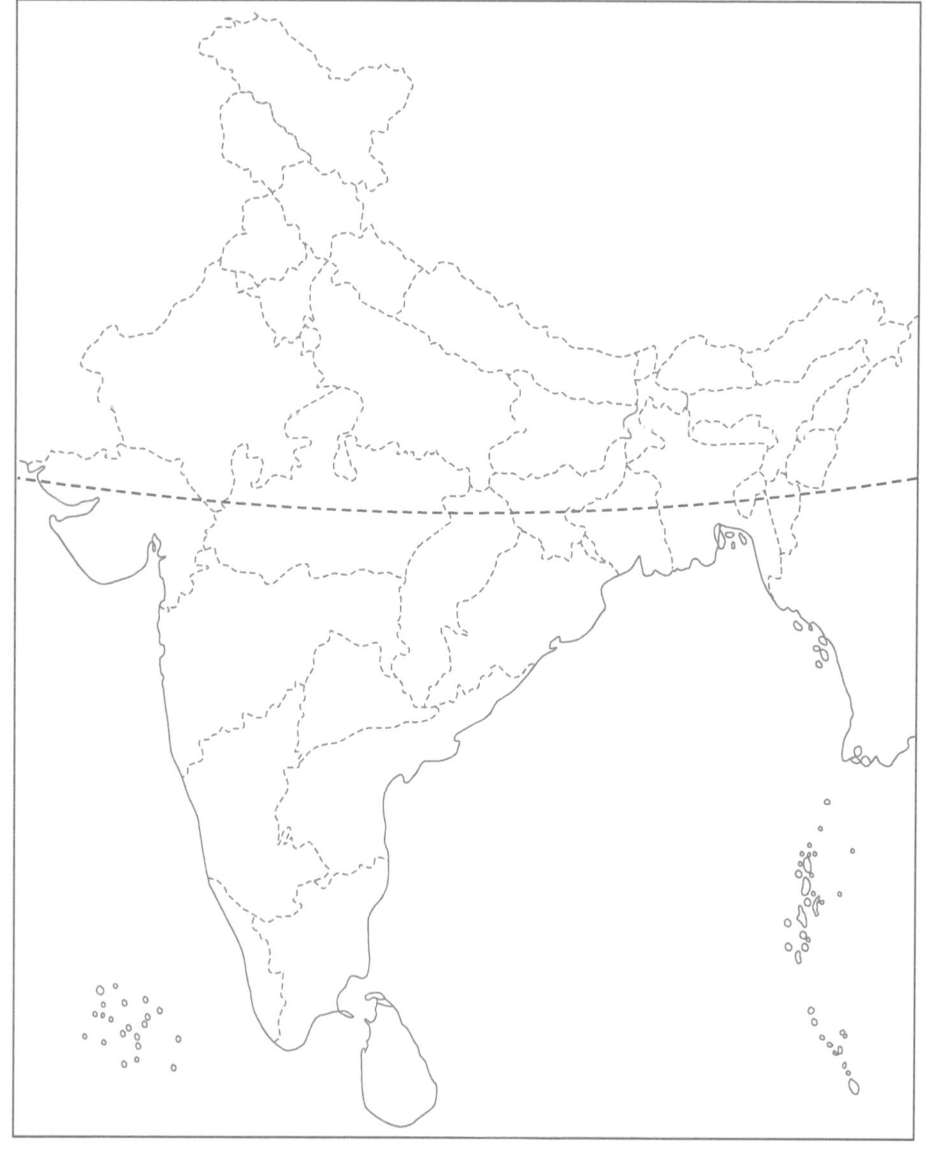

Practice Map 14

Q14 Locate and label the following items on the given map with appropriate symbols.

1 Namrup thermal power plant   2 Singrauli nuclear power plant

3 Ramagundam thermal power plant

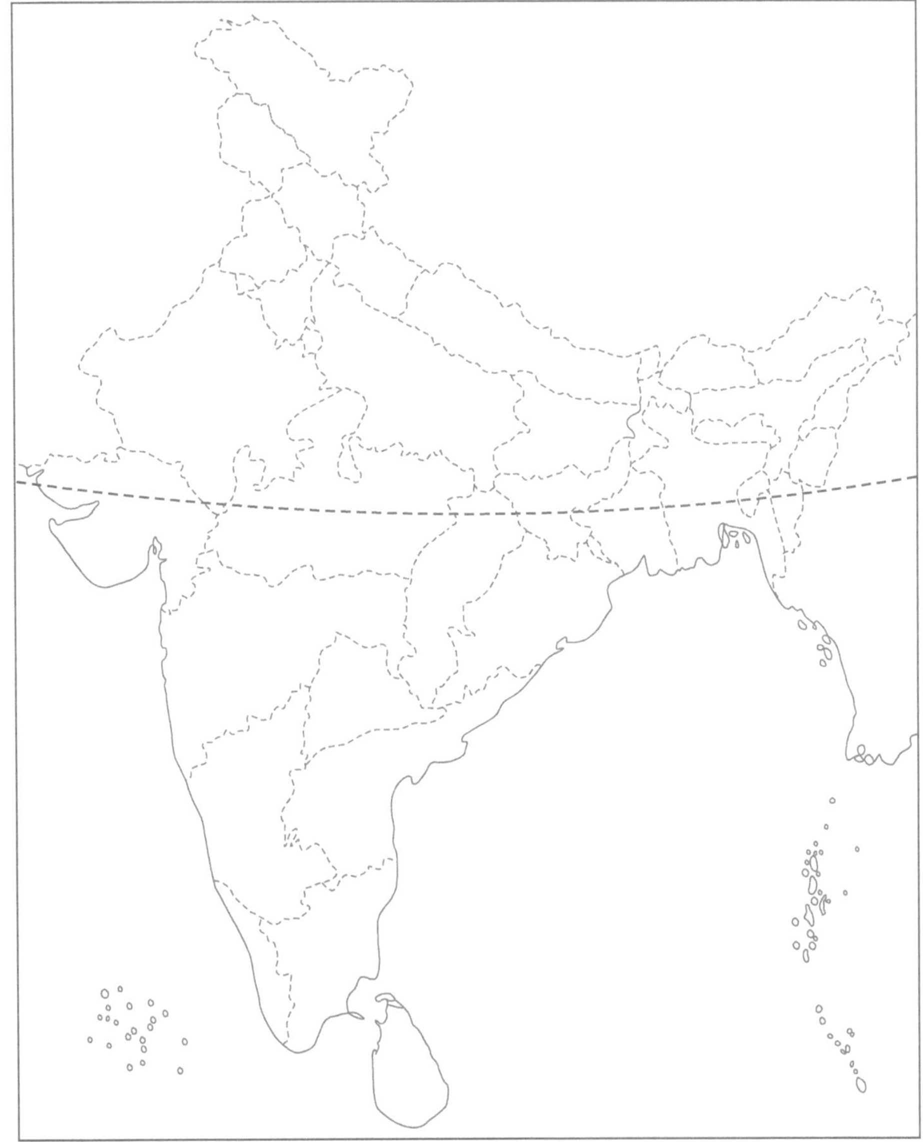

INDIA : Textile Industry of India
(Chapter-6 Manufacturing Industries)

This map shows the cotton, wollen and silk textile industries of India.

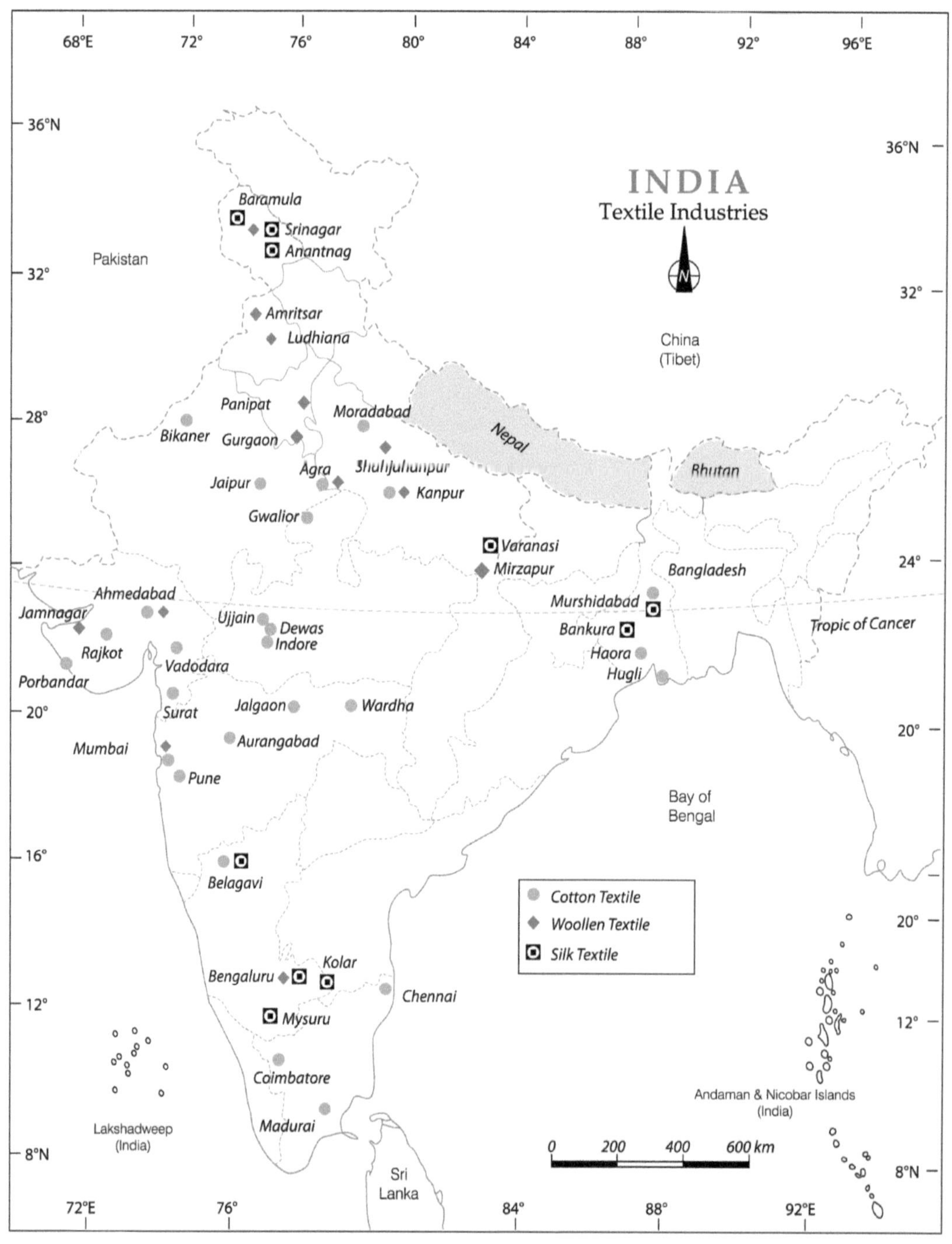

Practice Map 15

Q 15 Locate and label the following items on the given map with appropriate symbols.

1 Mumbai cotton textile industry
2 Indore cotton textile industry
3 Surat cotton textile industry
4 Kanpur cloth textile industry
5 Coimbatore cotton textile industry

[CBSE 2020]

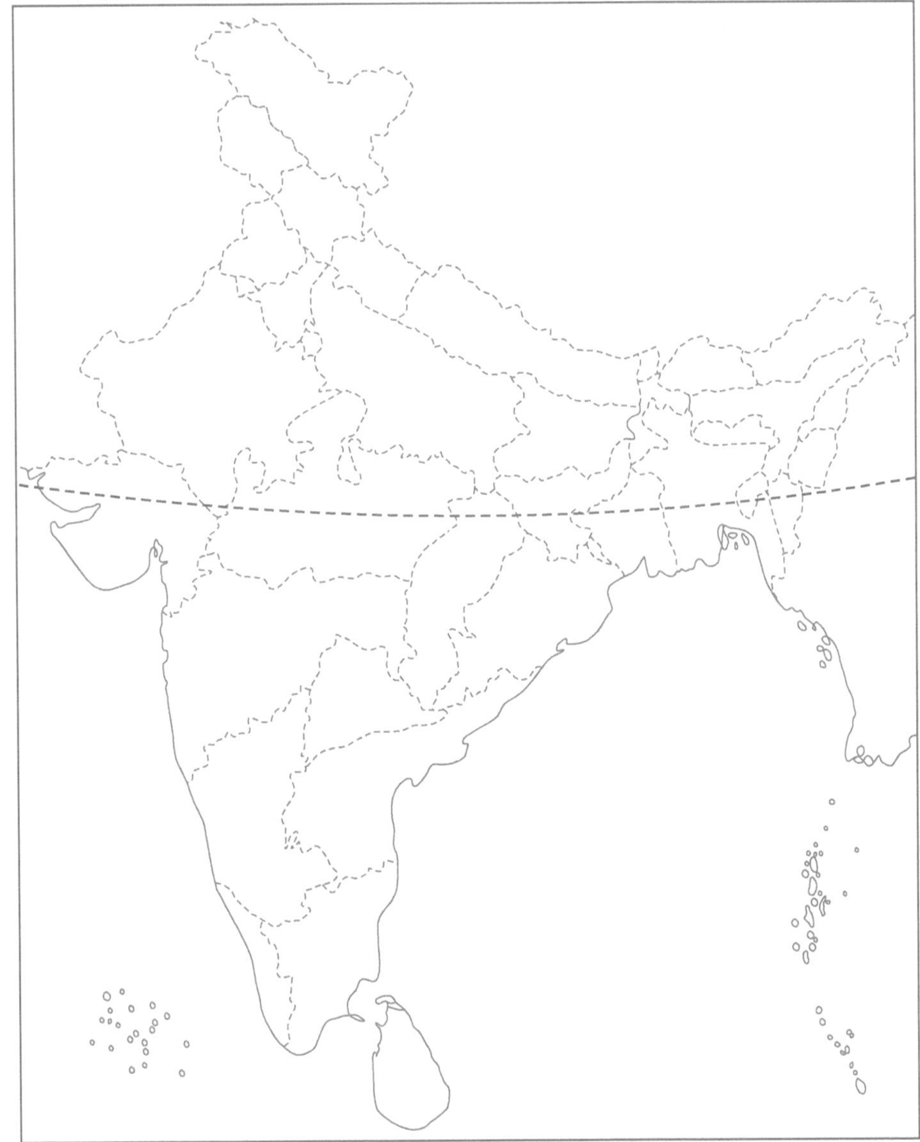

INDIA : Iron and Steel Industry of India
(Chapter-6 Manufacturing Industries)

This map shows the Iron and Steel Plants of India. Iron and Steel is a heavy industry because all the raw materials as well as finished goods are heavy and bulky.

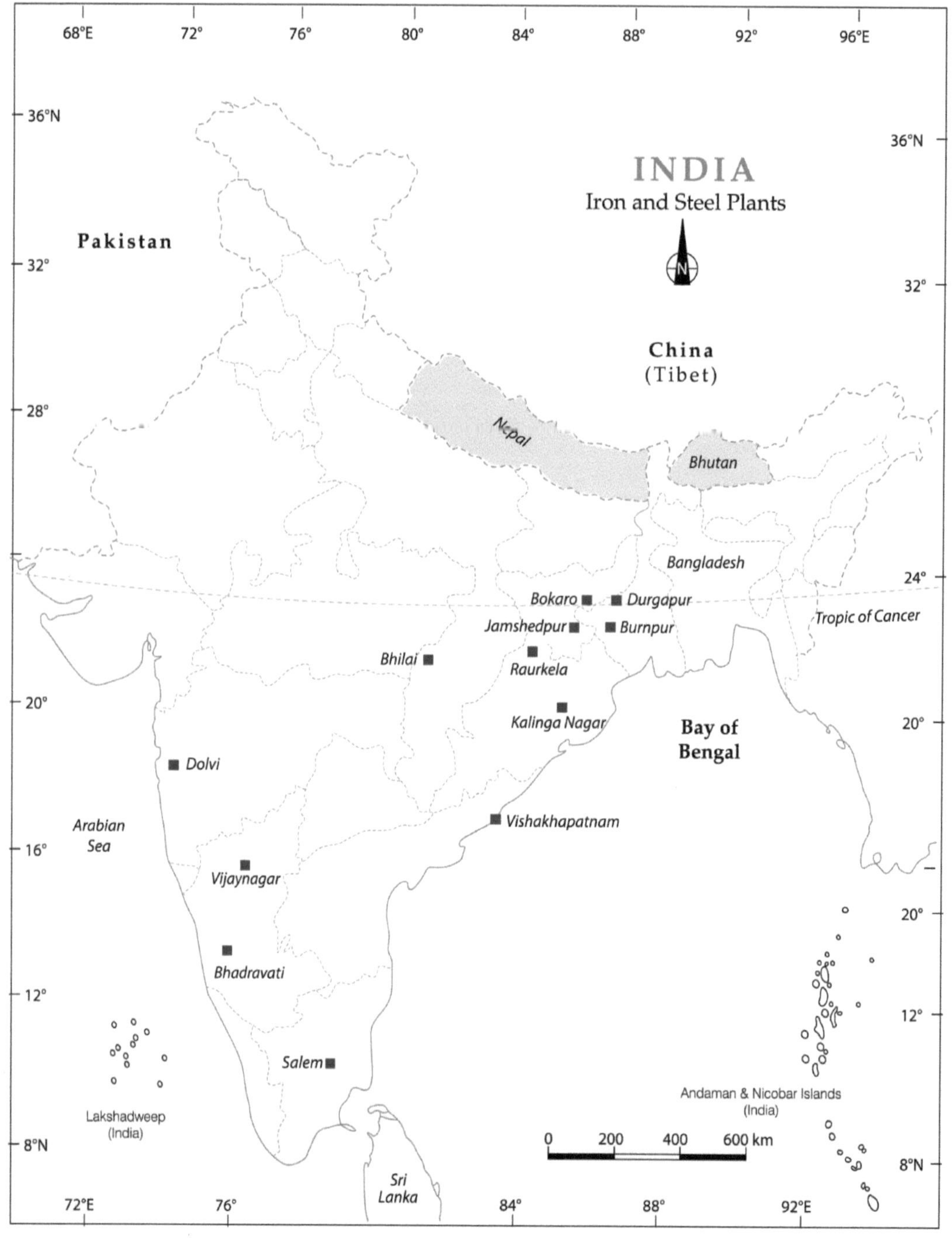

Practice Map 16

Q 16 Locate and label the following items on the given map with appropriate symbols.

1 Jamshedpur Iron and Steel Plant

2 Vijaynagar Iron and Steel Plant

3 Salem Iron and Steel Plant

4 Bokaro Iron and Steel Plant

5 Bhilai Iron and Steel Plant [CBSE 2020]

6 Durgapur Iron and Steel Plant

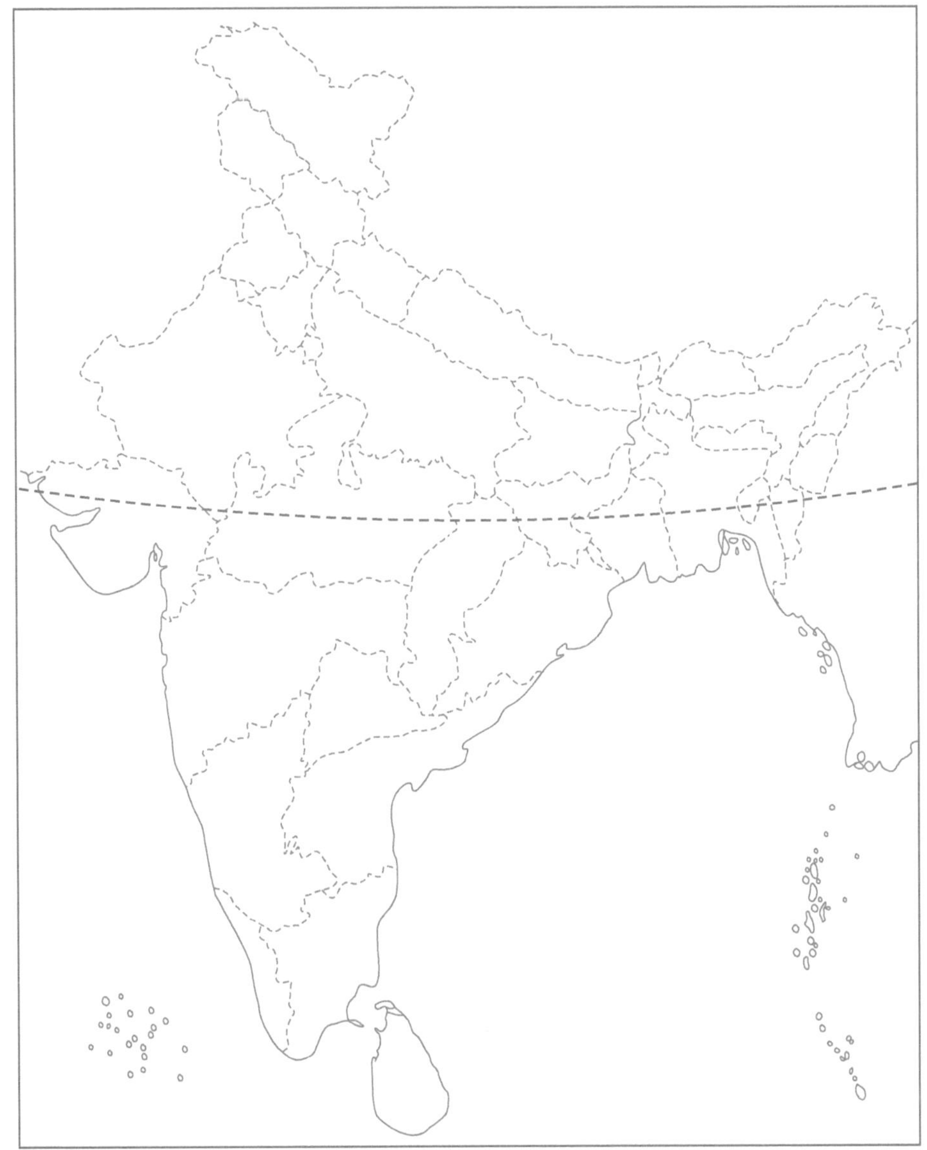

INDIA : Software Technology Park of India
(Chapter-6 Manufacturing Industries)

This map shows the software technology parks in India. Bengaluru is known as the electronic capital of India.

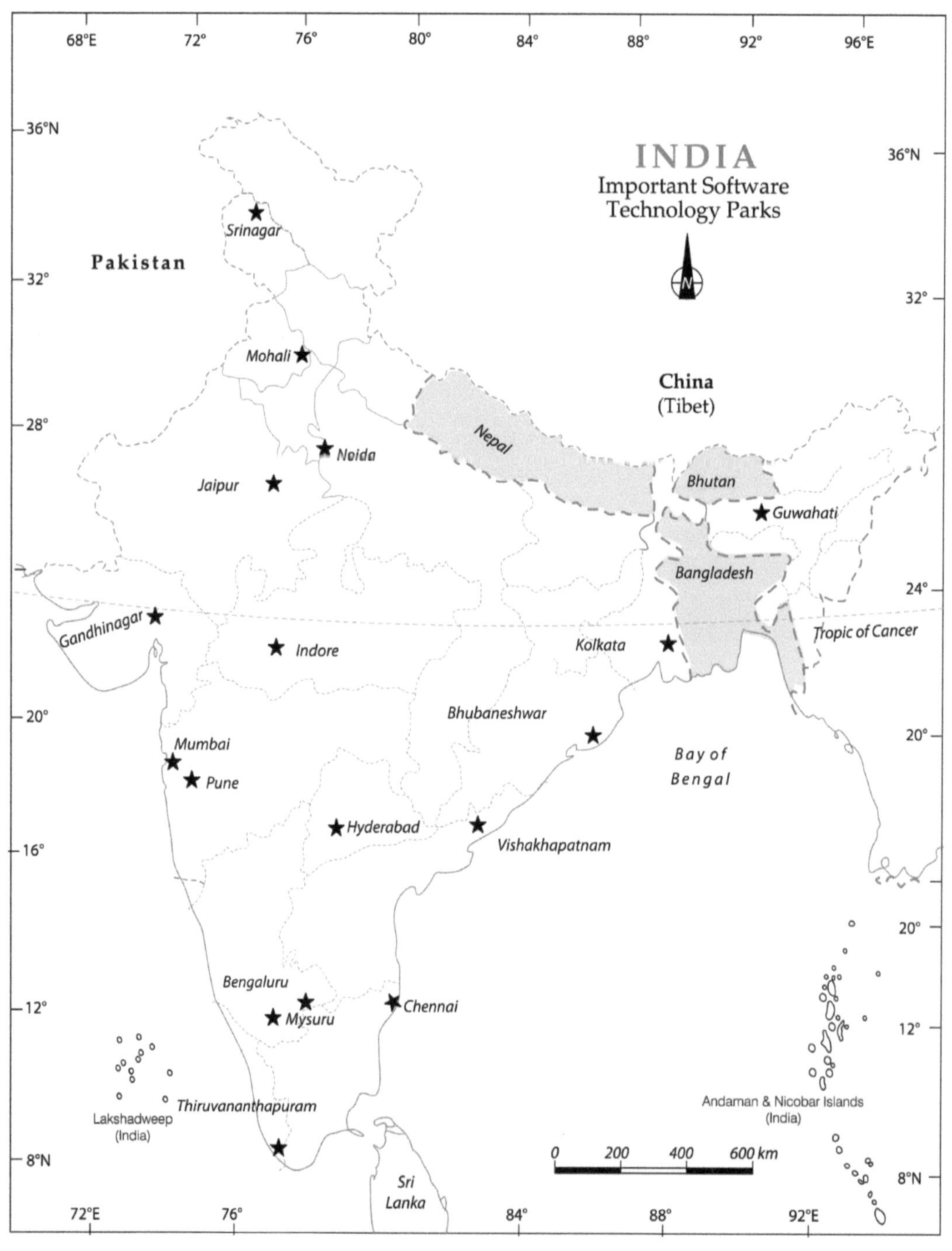

Practice Map 17

Q 17 Locate and label the following items on the given map with appropriate symbols.

1 Hyderabad Software Technology Park

2 Gandhinagar Software Technology Park

3 Mumbai Software Technology Park

4 Chennai Software Technology Park

5 Bengaluru Software Technology Park

6 Noida Software Technology Park

7 Pune Software Technology Park [CBSE 2020]

8 Thiruvananthapuram Software Technology Park

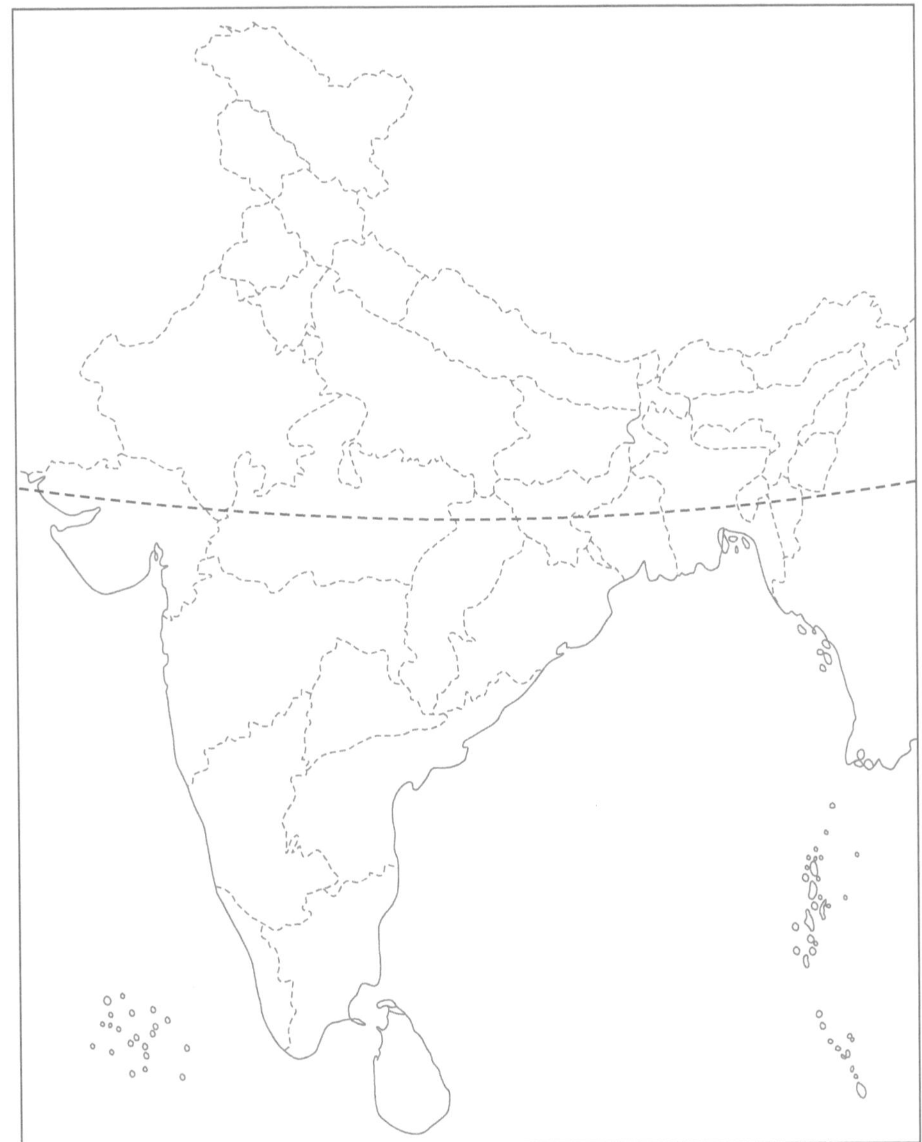

Major Seaports and International Airports of India
(Chapter-7 Lifelines of National Economy)

This map shows the major international airports and major seaports of India

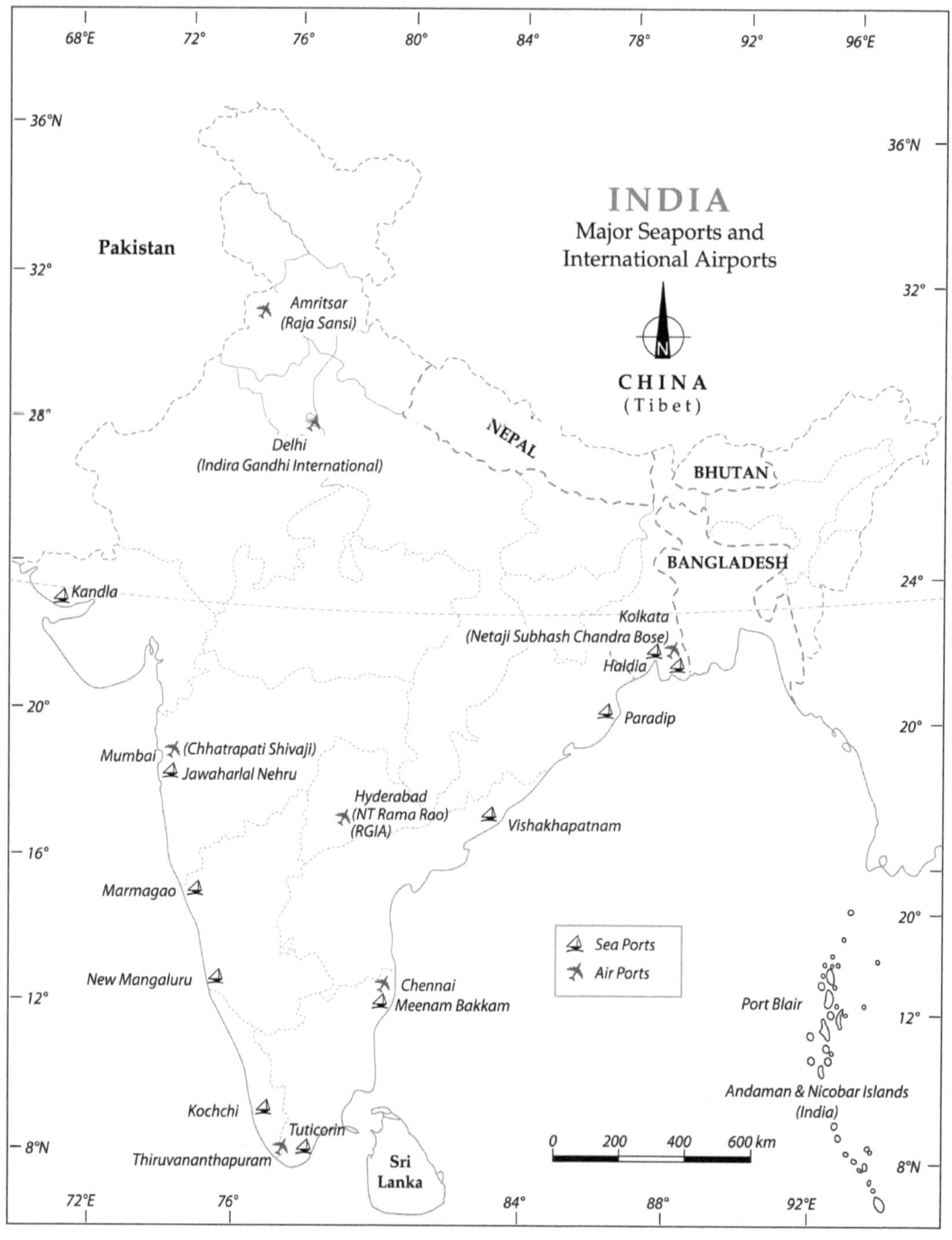

Practice Map 18

Q 18 On the given political map of India, name and locate the following

1. Netaji Subhash Chandra Bose Airport
2. Raja Sansi Airport
3. Meenam Bakkam International Airport
4. Indira Gandhi Airport
5. Chhatrapati Shivaji Airport
6. Rajiv Gandhi Airport

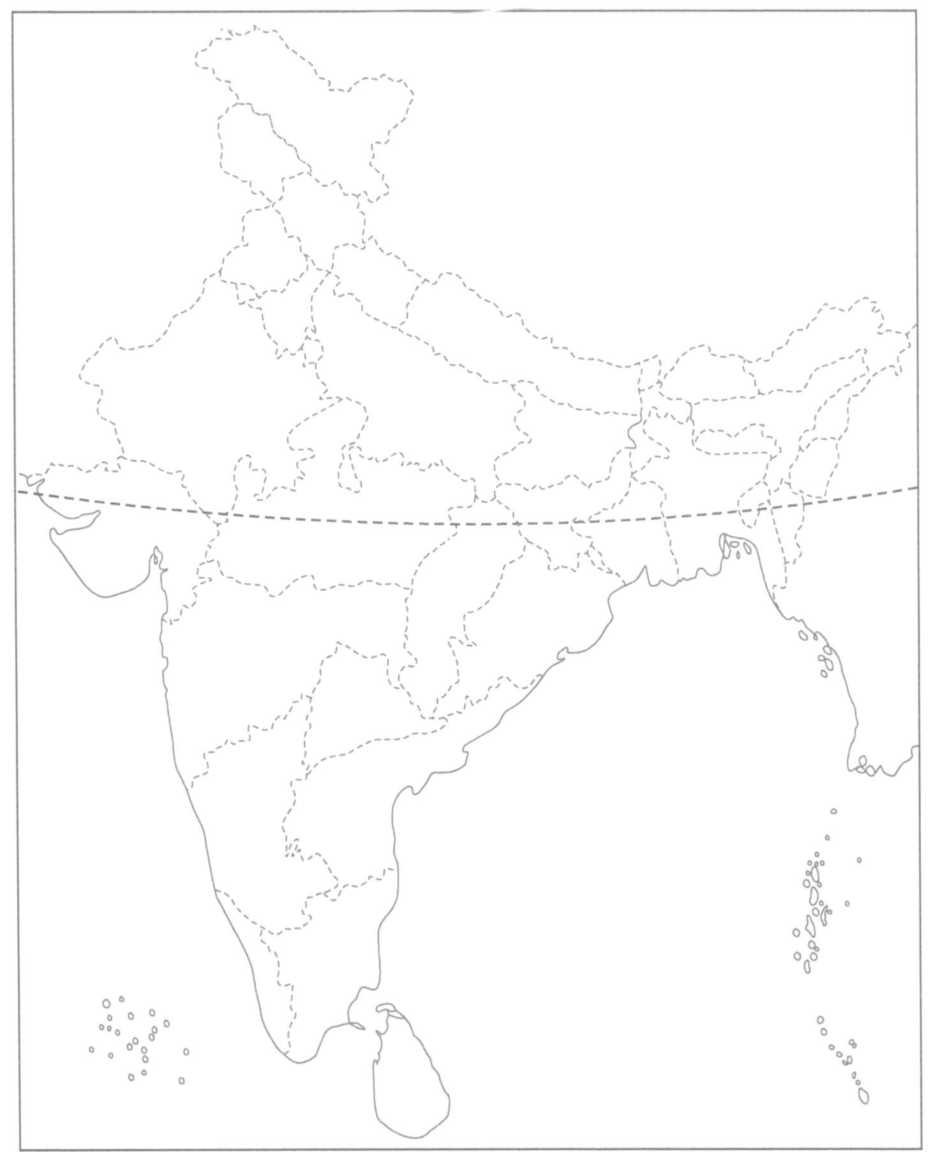

Practice Map 19

Q 19 Some major ports are marked by numbers in the given outline map of India as 1, 2, 3, 4, 5, 6, 7, 8, 9 and 10. Identify these features and write their correct names on the lines marked in the map.

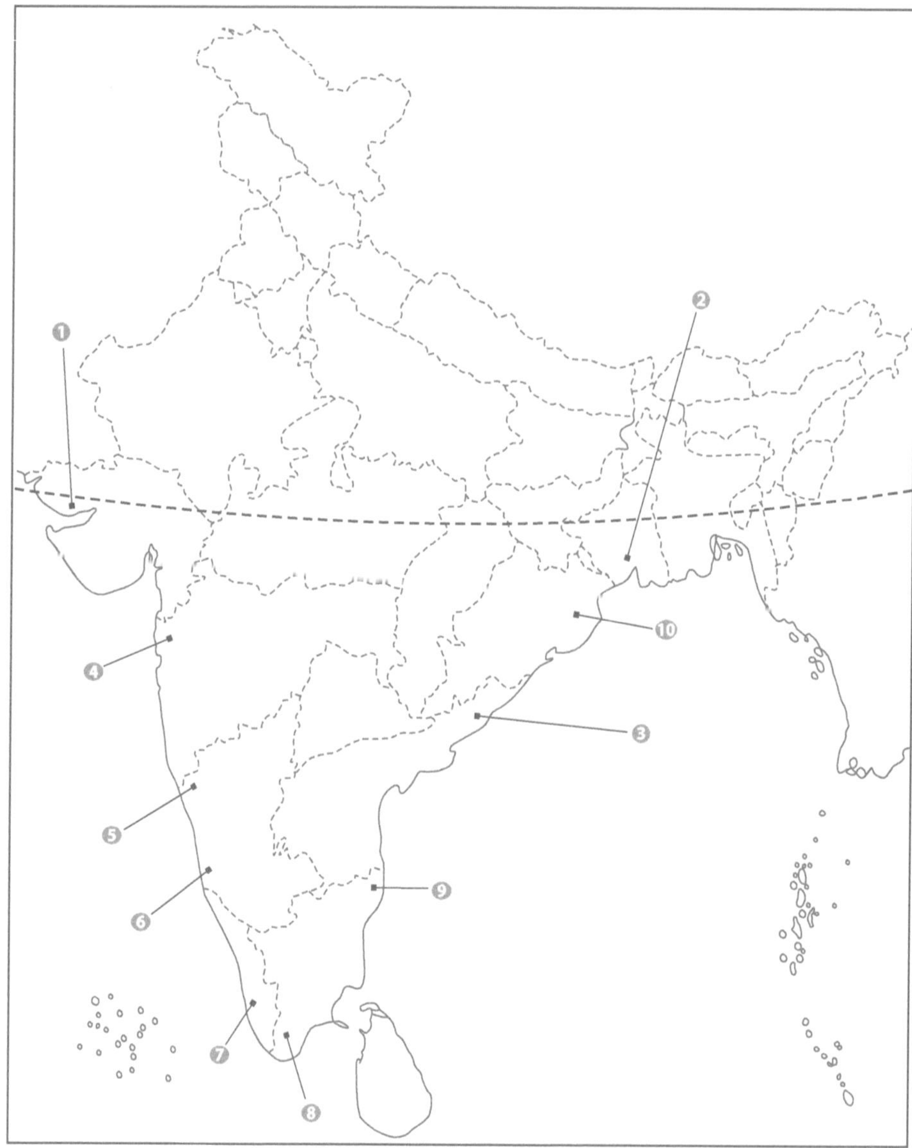

Exam Practice

Map 1

Q1 Some dams are marked by numbers in the given political outline map of India as 1, 2 and 3. Identify these features and write their correct names on the lines marked in the map.

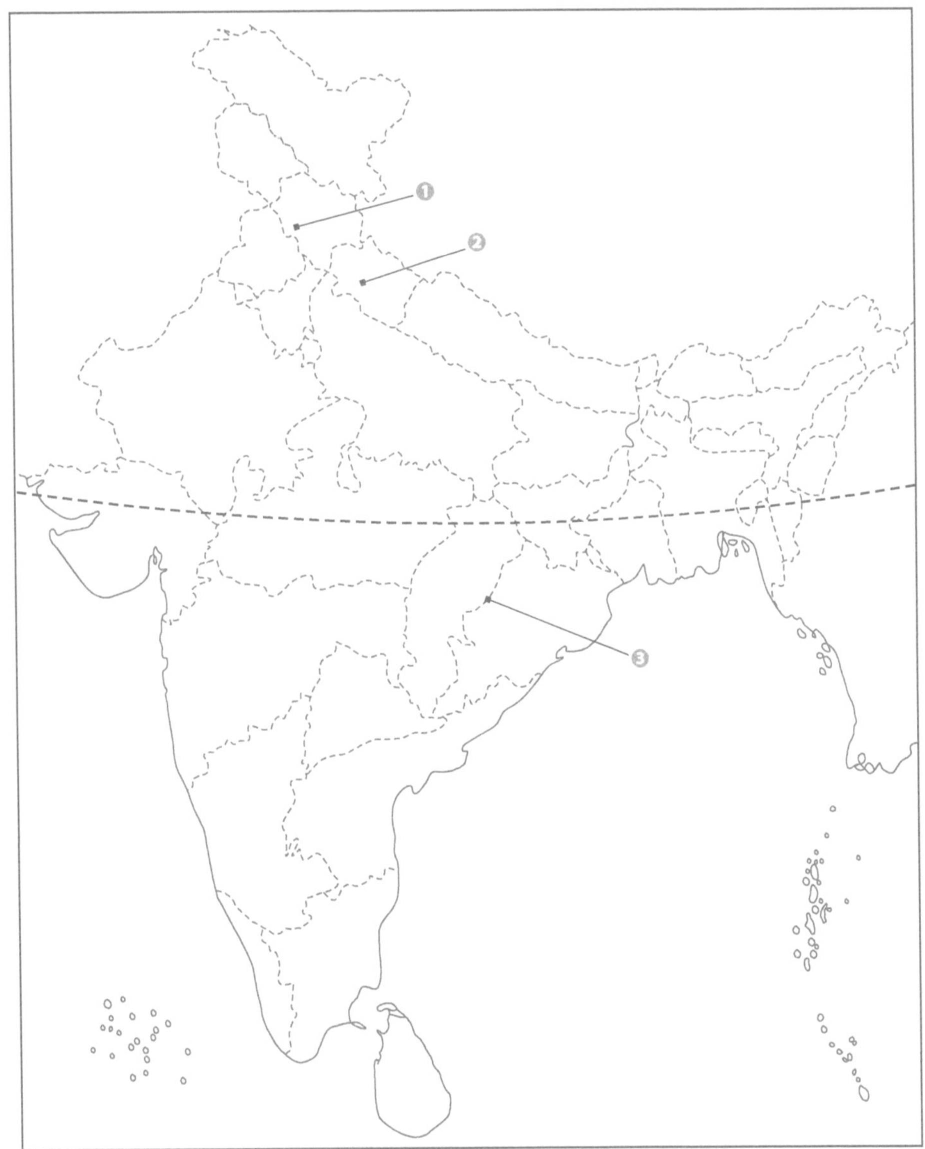

Map 2

 Features are marked by numbers in the given political map of India. Identify these features with the help of the following information and write their correct names on the lines marked in the map.

    1 Major wheat producing areas

    2 Major rice producing areas

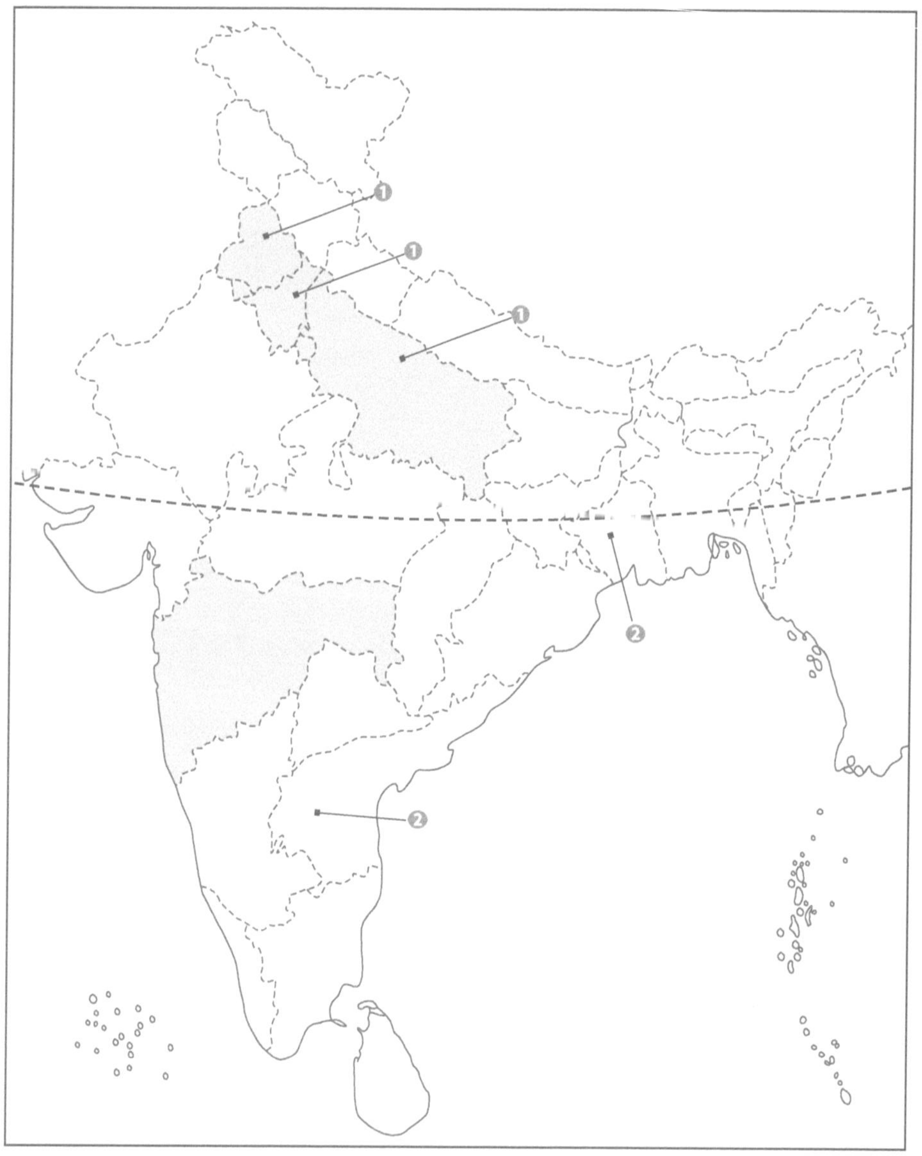

Map 3

Q3 Features are marked by number in the given political map of India. Identify these features with the help of the following information and write their correct names on the lines marked in the map.

  1 The leading jute or Golden Fibre producing state   [CBSE 2011, 10]

  2 Leading coffee producing state   [CBSE 2011, 10]

  3 Major sugarcane producing state   [CBSE 2010]

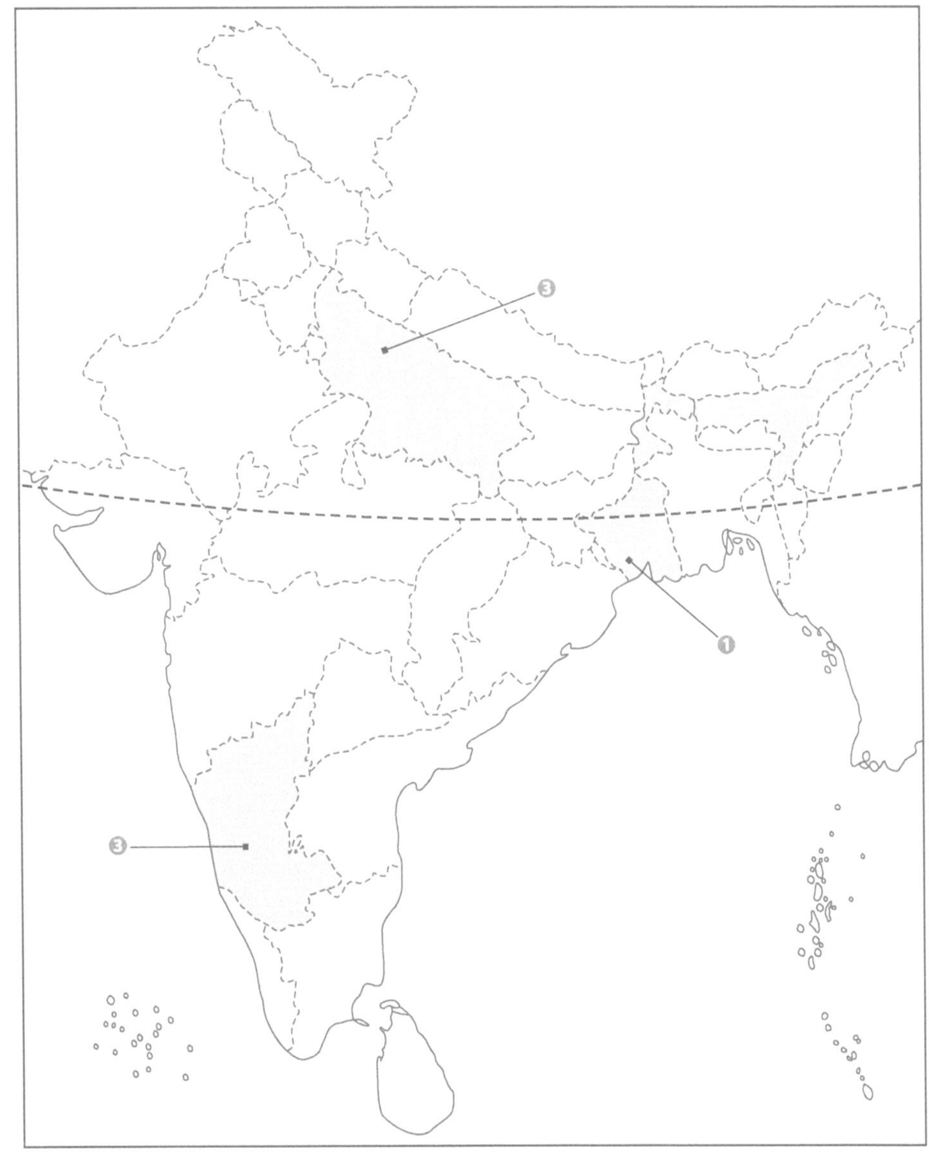

Map 4

Q4 Locate and label the following items on the given map with appropriate symbols.

1. Kakrapara nuclear power plant
2. Vishakhapatnam port
3. Bhilai iron and steel industry

[CBSE 2020]

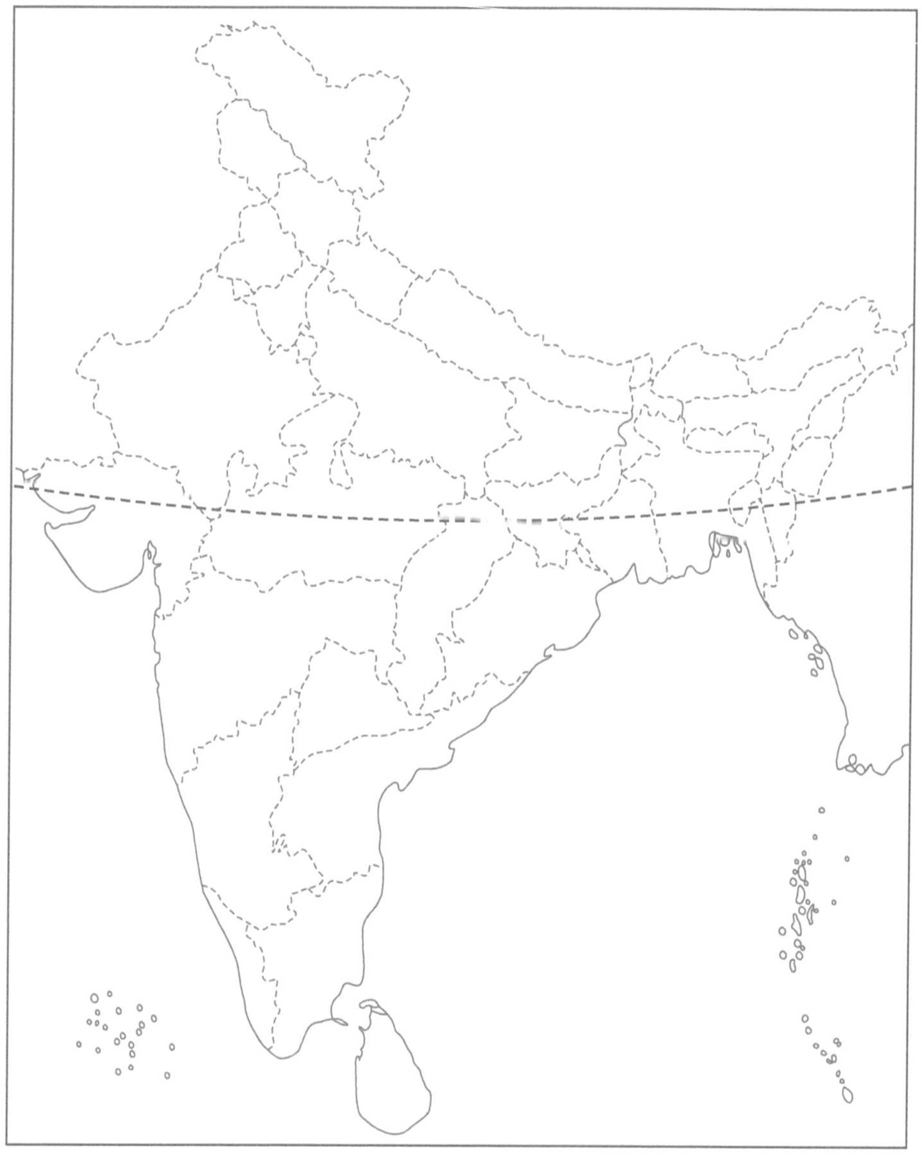

Map 5

Q5 Features are marked by numbers in the given political map of India. Identify these features with the help of the following information and write their correct names on the lines marked in the map.

  1 An oil field   2 A thermal power plant
  3 An iron ore mine

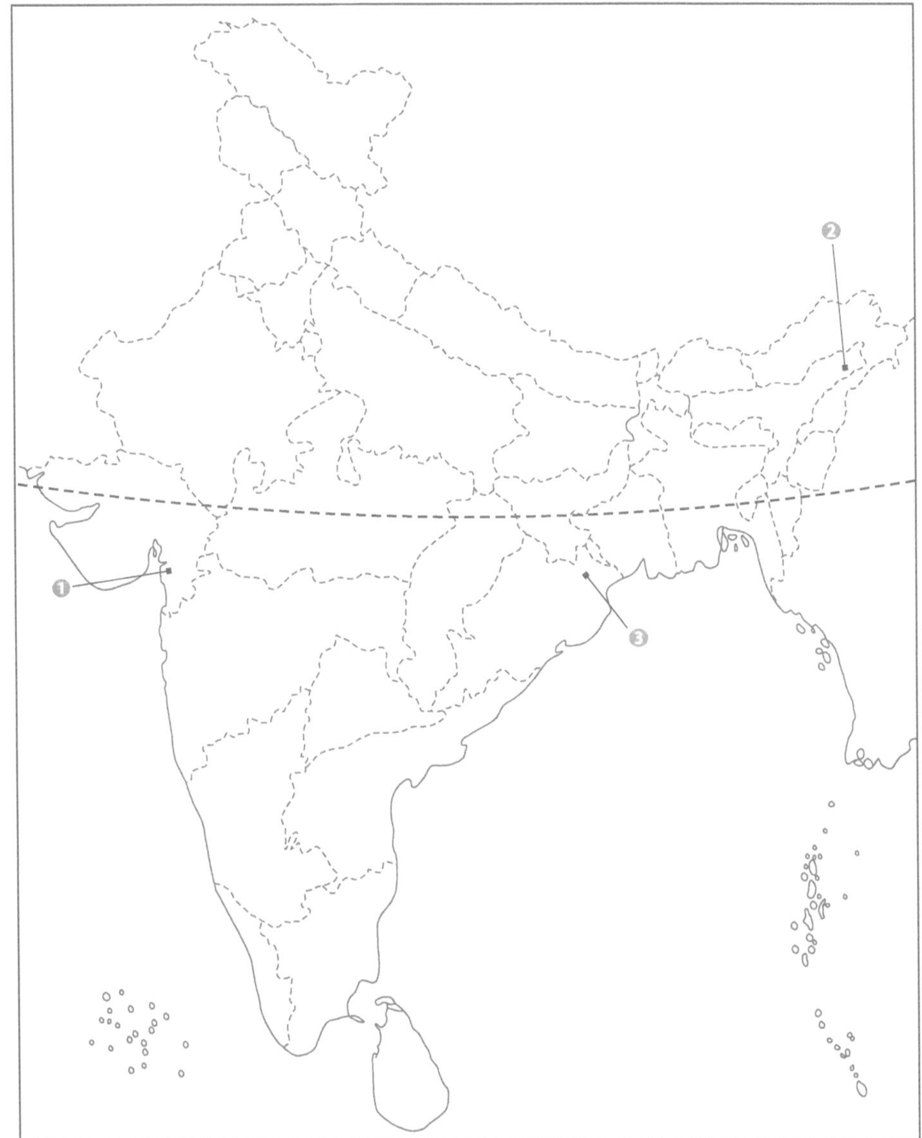

Map 6

Q 6 Locate and label the following items on the given map with appropriate symbols.

1 Bokaro iron and steel plant   2 Chennai software technology park
3 Indira Gandhi International airport

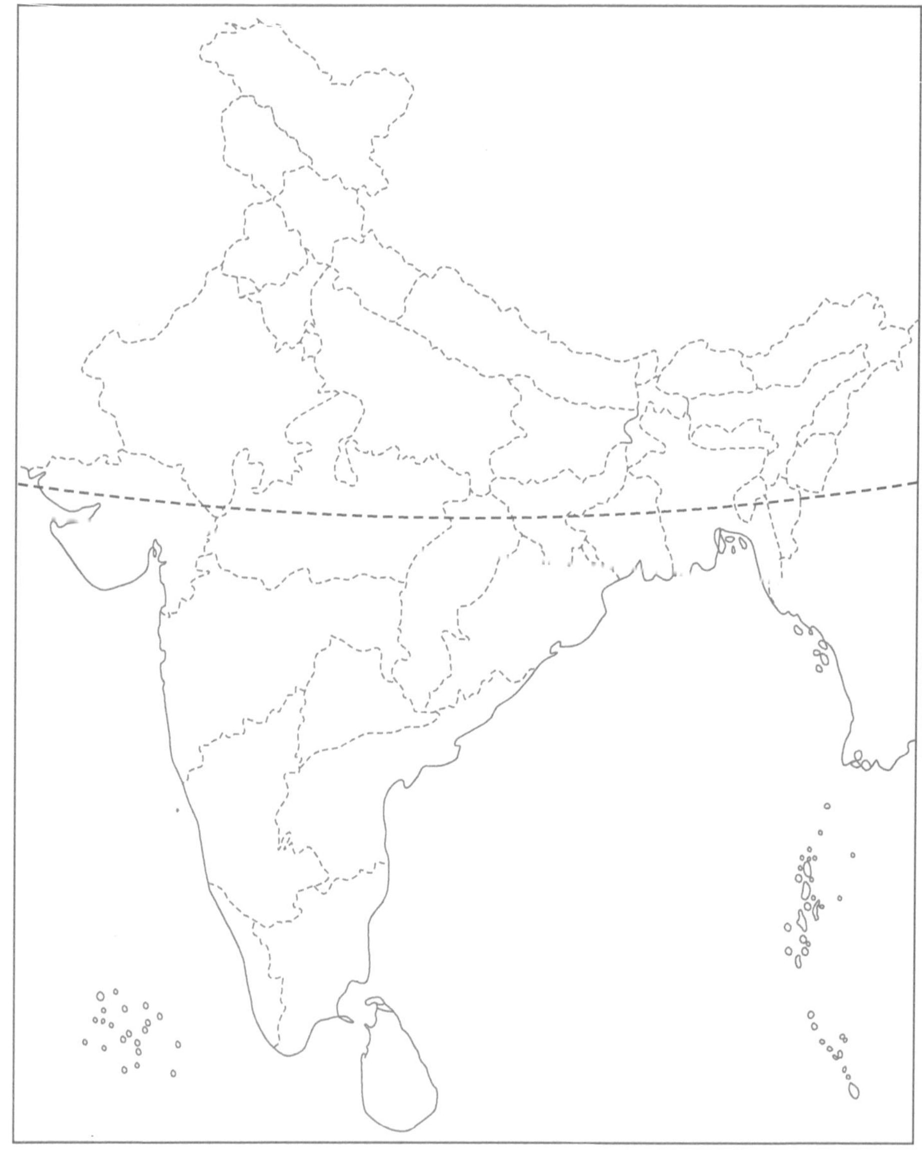

Answers (Practice Map)

Map 1

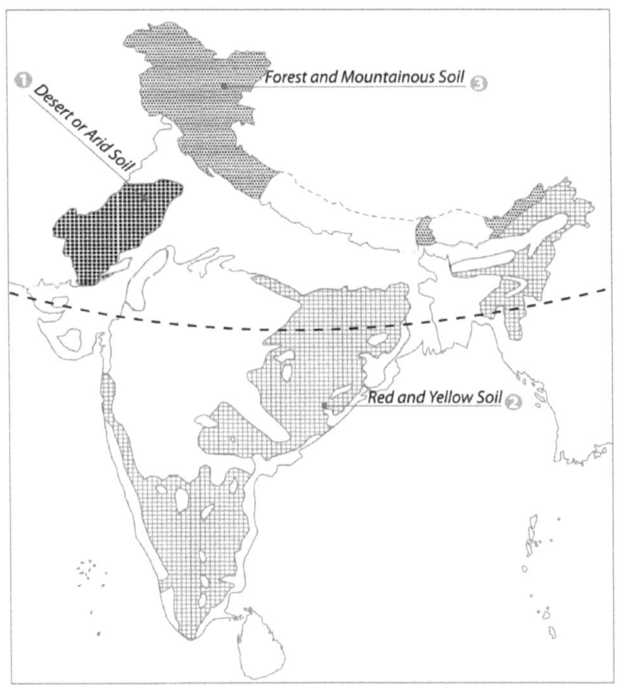

Map 2

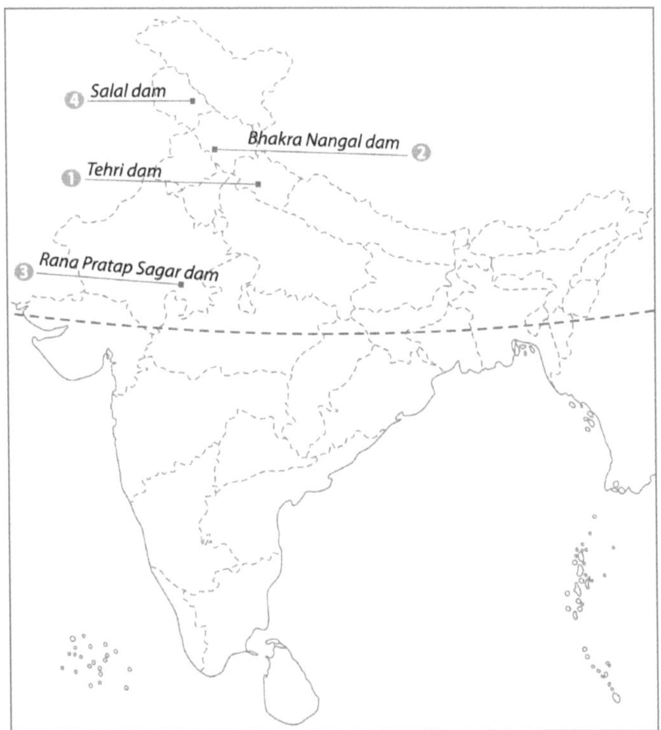

Map 3

Sardar sarovar dam
4
3 Hirakud dam
2 Nagarjuna Sagar dam
1
Tungabhadra dam

Map 4

2 Punjab
Haryana
3
Uttar Pradesh 1
Madhya Pradesh
4

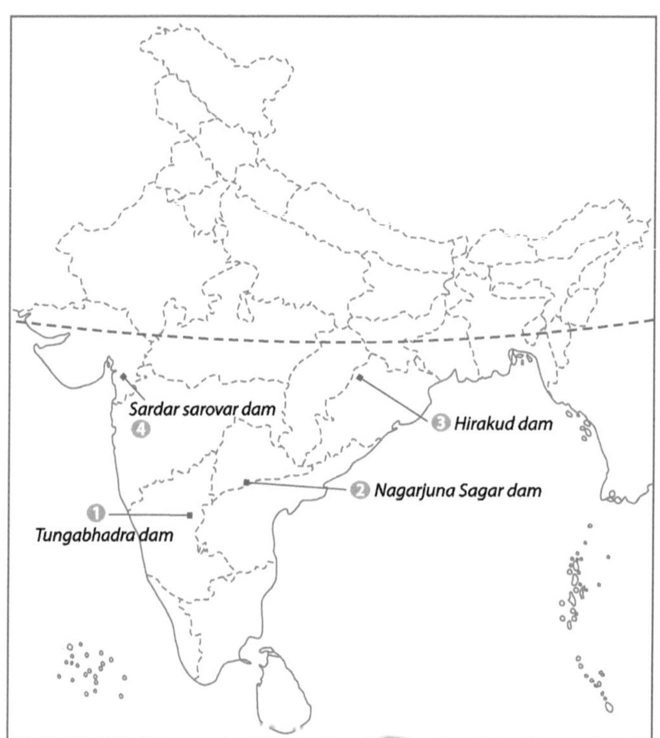

Map 5

Punjab
Uttar Pradesh
West Bengal
Andhra Pradesh

Map 6

Punjab
Uttar Pradesh
Haryana

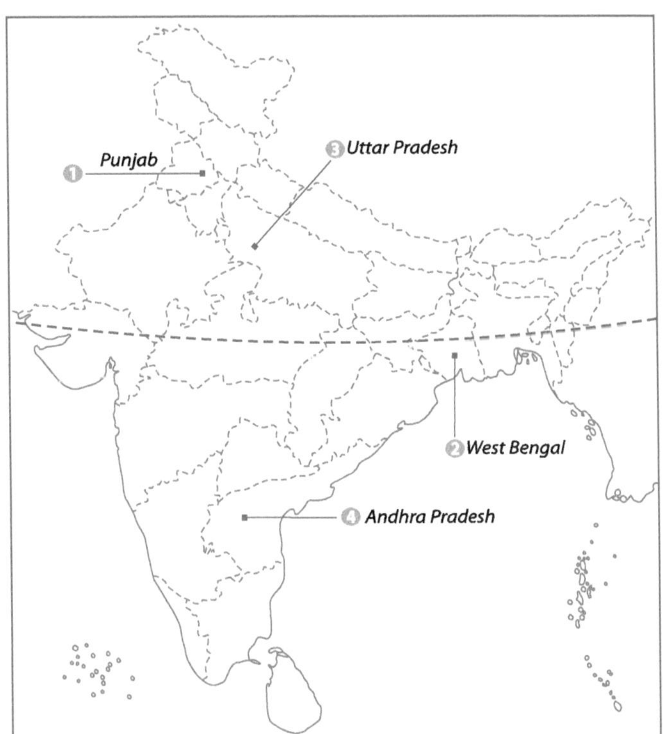

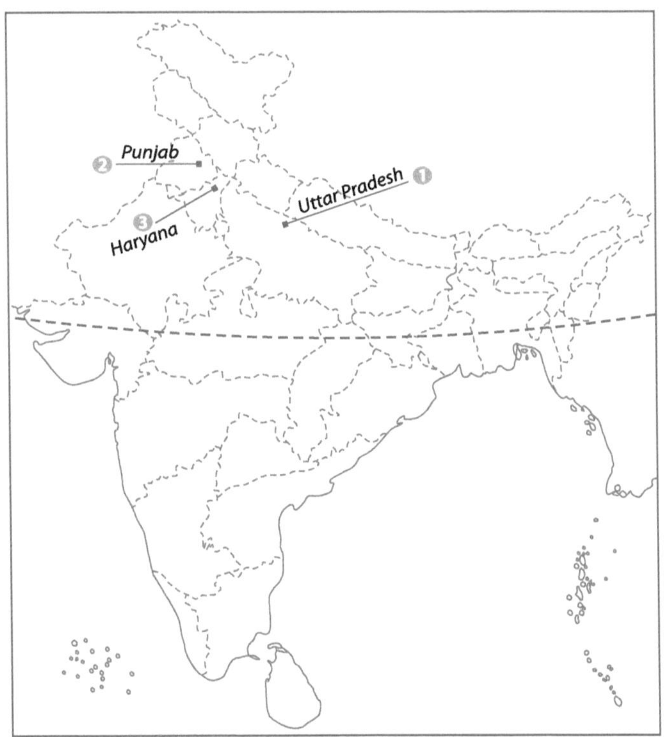

Map 7

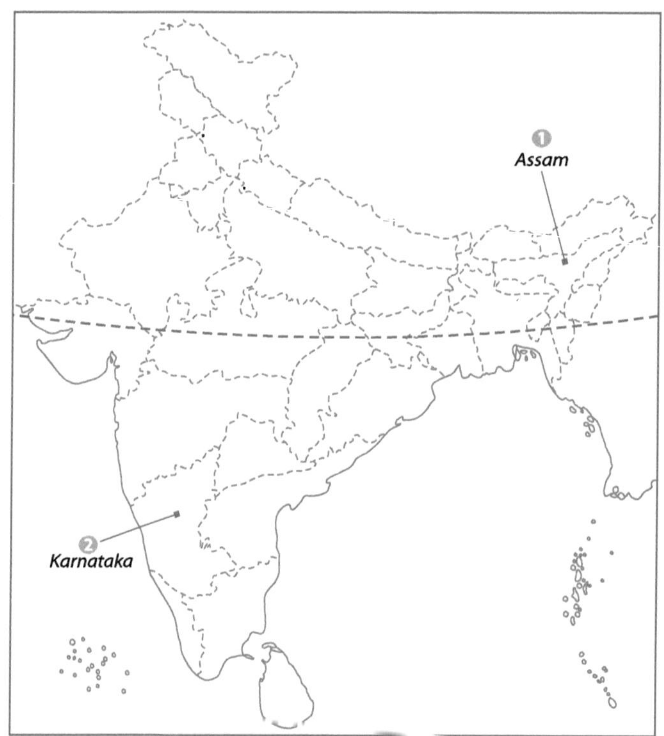

Map 8

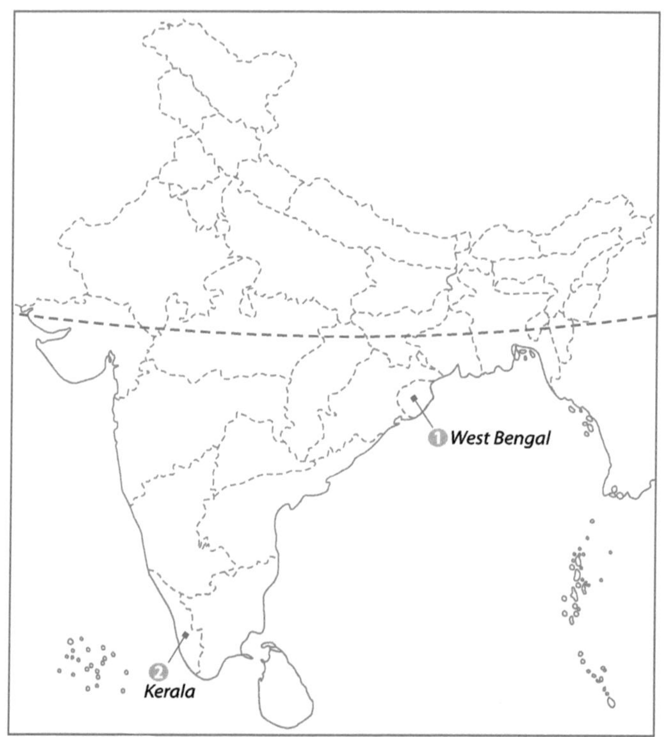

Map 9

Map 10

Map 11

Digboi 1
Naharkatia 2
5 Kolol
6
Ankaleshwar
4 Bassien
3
Mumbai
High

Map 12

1 Mayurbhanj
2 Durg
3 Bailadila
5
Kudramukh
4
Bellary

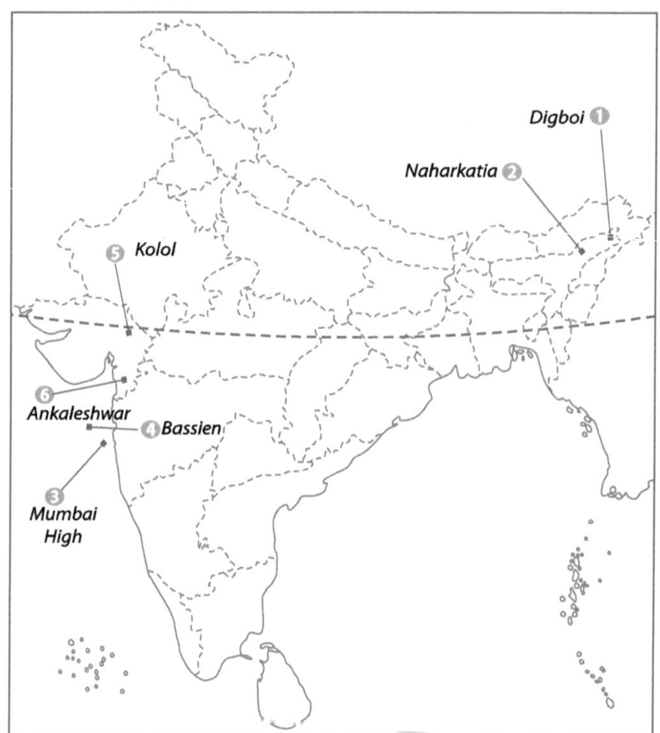

Map 13

Naraura
1
Kakrapara
4
3
Tarapur
Kalpakkam
2

Map 14

Singrauli
2
Namrup
1
3 Ramagundam

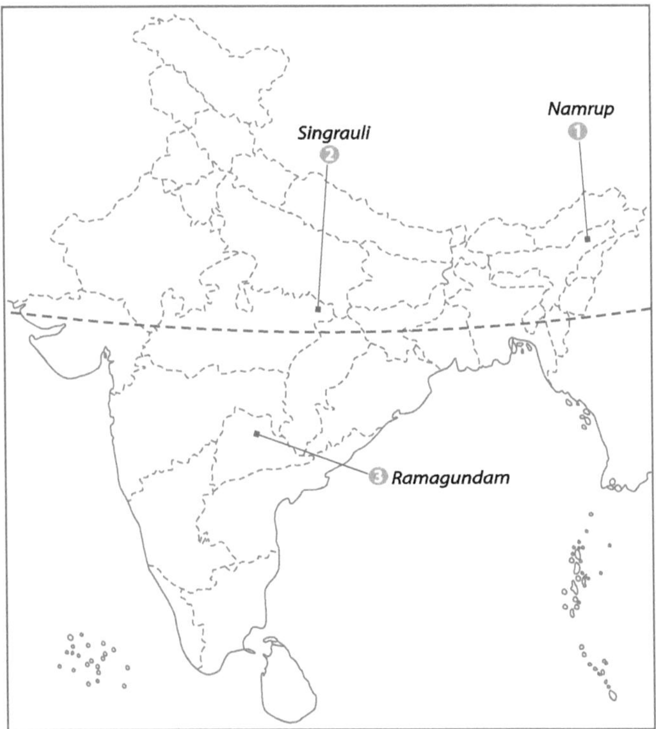

Map 15

Kanpur
Indore
Mumbai
Surat
Coimbatore

Map 16

Durgapur
Bokaro
Jamshedpur
Bhilai
Vijaynagar
Salem

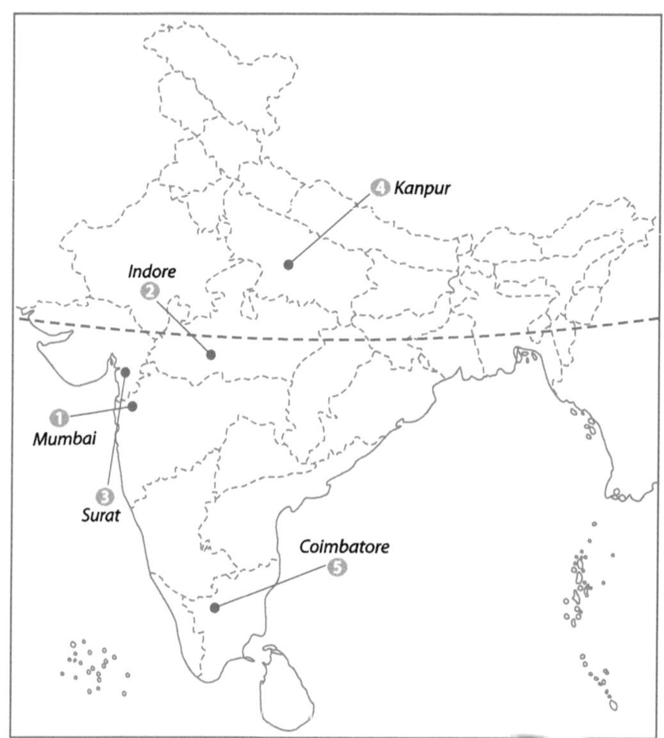

Map 17

⑥ Noida
② Gandhinagar
③ Mumbai
⑦ Pune
① Hyderabad
⑤ Bengaluru
④ Chennai
⑧ Thiruvananthapuram

Map 18

② Amritsar (Raja Sansi Airport)
④ Delhi (Indira Gandhi Airport)
⑤ Mumbai (Chhatrapati Shivaji Airport)
① Kolkata (Netaji Subhash Chandra Bose International Airport)
⑥ Hyderabad (Rajiv Gandhi Airport)
③ Chennai (Meenam Bakkam International Airport)

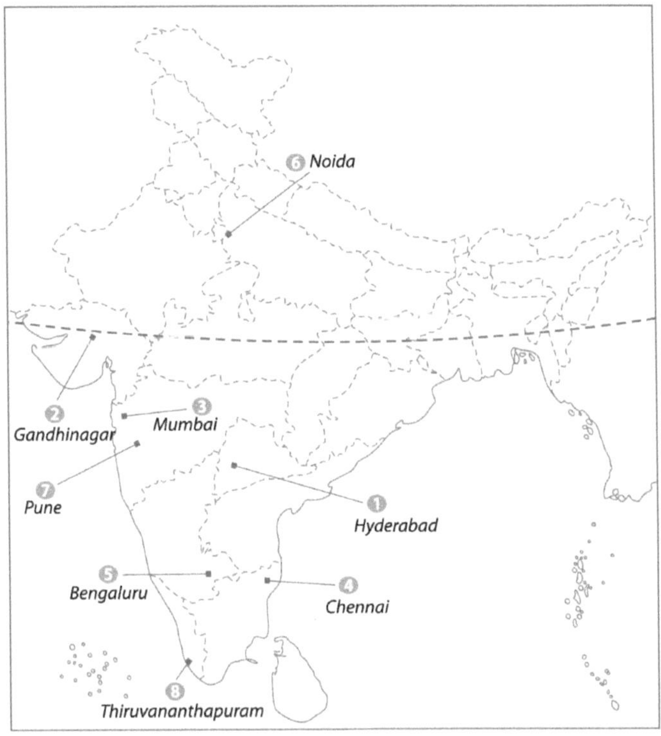

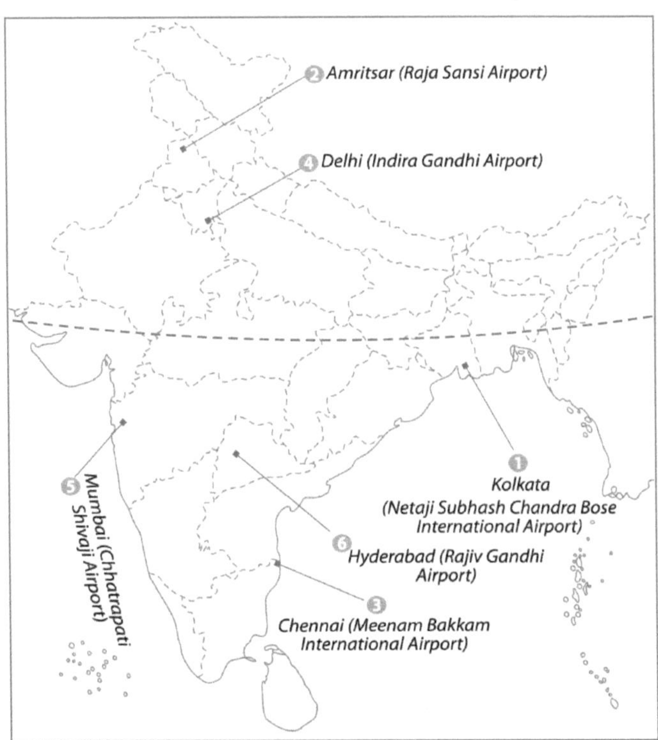

Map 19

Answers (Exam Practice)

Map 1

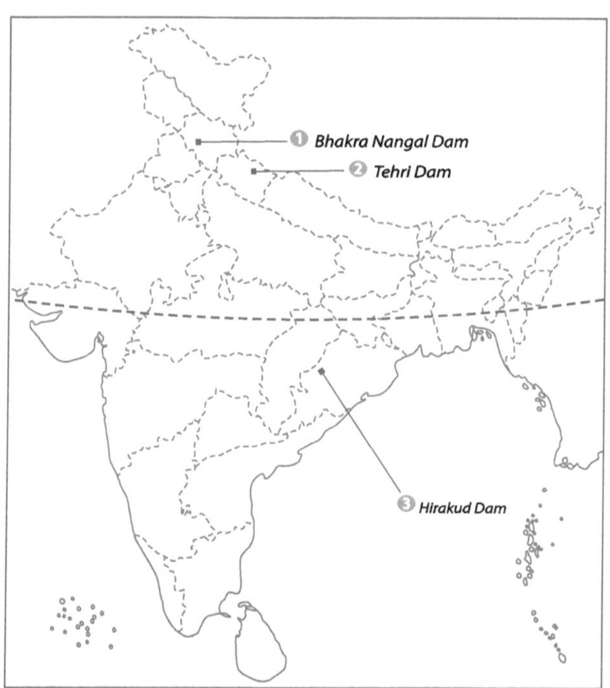

Map 2

Punjab 1
Haryana 1
Uttar Pradesh 1
West Bengal 2
2 Andhra Pradesh

Map 3

Uttar Pradesh 3
1
West Bengal
2 Karnataka

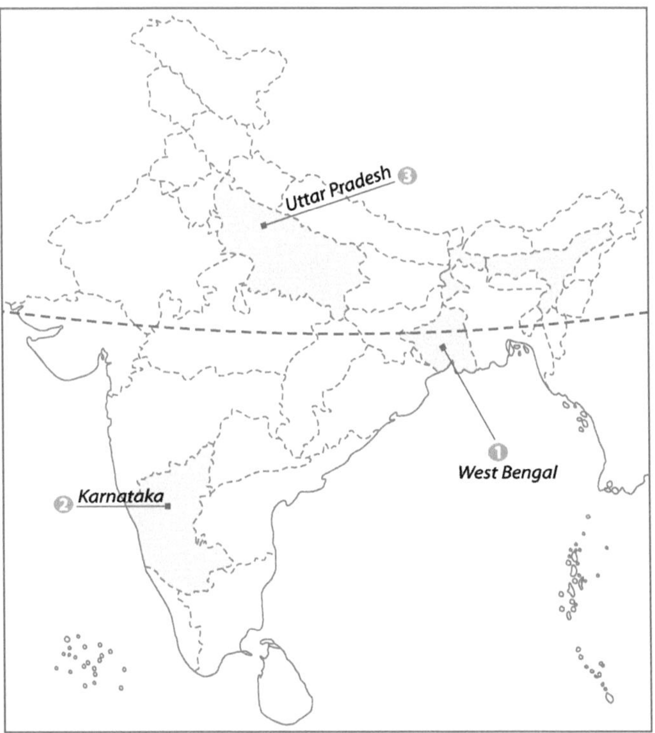

Map 4

Bhilai iron and steel industry
Kakrapara
Vishakhapatnam port

Map 5

Namrup
Ankaleshwar
Mayurbhanj

Map 6

Printed by Libri Plureos GmbH in Hamburg,
Germany